Holy Scripture

MW00638099

May we speak, in the present age, of *Holy* Scripture? And what validation of that claim can be offered, robust enough to hold good for both religious practice and intellectual inquiry?

John Webster argues that while any understanding of Scripture must subject it to proper textual and historical interrogation, it is necessary at the same time to acknowledge the special character of scriptural writing. He examines terms such as 'revelation', 'sanctification' and 'inspiration' in relation to Scripture and in doing so finds that there is a way to counter the tendency of modern culture to bifurcate the transcendent reality of God and the material texts of the Bible.

This book is an exercise in Christian dogmatics, a loud reaffirmation of the triune God at the heart of a Scripture-based Christianity. But it is written with intellectual rigour by a theologian who understands the currents of modern secular thought and is able to work from them towards a constructive position on biblical authority. It will resonate with anyone who has wondered or worried about the grounds on which we may validly regard the Bible as God's direct communication with humanity.

JOHN WEBSTER is Professor of Systematic Theology, University of Aberdeen. He is the editor of the *International Journal of Systematic Theology*.

CURRENT ISSUES IN THEOLOGY

General Editor:

Iain Torrance
Professor in Patristics and Christian Ethics, Master of Christ's College, and Dean of the Faculty of Arts & Divinity, University of Aberdeen

Editorial Advisory Board:

David Ford *University of Cambridge*
Bryan Spinks *Yale University*
Kathryn Tanner *University of Chicago*
John Webster *University of Aberdeen*

There is a need among upper-undergraduate and graduate students of theology, as well as among Christian teachers and church professionals, for a series of short, focussed studies of particular key topics in theology written prominent theologians. *Current Issues in Theology* meets this need.

The books in the series are designed to provide a 'state-of-the-art' statement on the topic in question, engaging with contemporary thinking as well providing original insights. The aim is to publish books which stand between the static monograph genre and the more immediate statement of a journal article, by authors who are questioning existing paradigms or rethinking perspectives.

Other title in the series:

The Just War Revisited Oliver O'Donovan

Holy Scripture

A Dogmatic Sketch

JOHN WEBSTER

CAMBRIDGE UNIVERSITY PRESS
Cambridge, New York, Melbourne, Madrid, Cape Town, Singapore, São Paulo,
Delhi, Dubai, Tokyo

Cambridge University Press
The Edinburgh Building, Cambridge, CB2 8RU, UK

Published in the United States of America by Cambridge University Press, New York

www.cambridge.org
Information on this title: www.cambridge.org/9780521538466

First published 2003
Seventh printing 2010

Printed in the United Kingdom at the University Press, Cambridge

A catalogue record for this publication is available from the British Library

Library of Congress Cataloguing in Publication data
Webster, John.
Holy Scripture: a dogmatic sketch / John Webster.
   p.   cm. – (Current issues in theology; v. 1)
Includes bibliographical references and index.
ISBN 0 521 83118 0 – ISBN 0 521 53846 7 (pbk.)
1. Bible – Evidences, authority, etc.   I. Title.   II. Series.
BS480.W39   2003
220.1′3 – dc21   2003046264

ISBN 978-0-521-83118-5 hardback
ISBN 978-0-521-53846-6 paperback

In Memoriam
Colin Gunton
1941–2003

Contents

Introduction   *page* 1

1 Revelation, sanctification and inspiration   5

2 Scripture, church and canon   42

3 Reading in the economy of grace   68

4 Scripture, theology and the theological school   107

   In place of a conclusion   136

   Bibliography   138

   Index   143

Introduction

What follows is a dogmatic sketch of a topic much neglected in contemporary theology, namely, the nature of Holy Scripture. It is only a sketch, not a treatise, and many issues which ought properly to be considered in a full account – the relation of Scripture and tradition, or of Scripture and preaching, for example – do not receive treatment. I am also conscious that I have little to say about topics which are very fully discussed in modern theology and hermeneutics. I offer no theory of 'textuality', and say almost nothing about such matters as the impact of deconstruction or of speech-act theory on thinking about the nature of Scripture, or the workings of interpretative communities. Whether these omissions are deficiencies I leave to the reader's judgement. The subjects to which I have addressed myself are chosen because they appear to me to constitute the essential articles of an orderly dogmatic account of what Holy Scripture is.

But *is* there such a thing as Holy Scripture? Theorists in cultural and religious studies, and more than a handful of modern theologians, seek to persuade us that there is not: that the term 'Holy Scripture' is an extension of the term 'scripture', and refers not to properties which the biblical canon has by virtue of its relation to God's communicative activity, but to the activities of human agents in constituting a cultural and religious world. Because what follows is an essay not in cultural or religious studies but in Christian dogmatics, it proposes that there is, indeed, such a thing as Holy Scripture, for the depiction of which we must deploy language of the triune God's saving and revelatory action. This dogmatic depiction does not deny that Holy Scripture is also a field of cultural invention, since Holy

Scripture (the human text which God sanctifies for the service of his communicative presence) is still 'scripture' (human writing generated and used by religious communities). But dogmatics does not allow the particular concept of 'Holy Scripture' to be folded into the more general category of 'scripture', preferring to maximise the differences between the two and thereby to resist the subordination of Holy Scripture to cultural poetics. The result is a dogmatic ontology of Holy Scripture: an account of what Holy Scripture *is* in the saving economy of God's loving and regenerative self-communication.

Dogmatics lies at the periphery of modern Anglo-American Protestant divinity, and I am acutely aware both that what many of my contemporaries regard as self-evident I find to be puzzling or unpersuasive and that matters which I regard as self-evident make many of my contemporaries feel bewildered. I console myself with the fact that I can find good company in some of my forbears. In 1935, Günther Dehn, who two years previously had been ejected from his chair in Practical Theology in Halle, gave a rather startling set of Dale lectures in Oxford under the title *Man and Revelation*. His hearers were certainly startled: in his preface to the published version, Dehn remembers the gentle head-shaking of the audience,[1] and goes on to say:

> I have endeavoured to deal with certain questions of Christian thought and life, not as a free scholar but as a theologian bound to the Church. This must seem strange to those who are told that theology is to be ranked among the branches of general knowledge, and that its problems can be treated in the same manner as those in other branches of spiritual knowledge, i.e. in accordance with the cultural consciousness of the age. The theologian most assuredly participates

[1] See G. Dehn, *Man and Revelation* (London: Hodder & Stoughton, 1936), p. 8; in his foreword to the book, Nathaniel Micklem, then Principal of Mansfield College, under whose auspices the Dale lectures were offered, notes somewhat wryly that 'I cannot anticipate that this book will win full acceptance from English-speaking Christians' (p. 3).

in the cultural consciousness of his time, but for his work this has none but formal significance. Theology is not promoted by culture but by the belief in God's revelation as an event beyond all human history, to which Scripture bears witness and which finds confirmation in the Confessions of our Church. Only a theology that clings inexorably to these most essential presuppositions can help build up a Church that really stands unshaken amidst all the attacks of the spirit of the age. And such a Church alone will be the salt of the earth and the light of the world; any other Church will perish along with the world.[2]

Rem acu tetigisti.

A dogmatic account of the nature of Holy Scripture can, of course, have only a modest role, ancillary to the primary theological task, which is exegesis. The clarifications which such an account can offer are not without their significance, articulating as they do the exegete's understanding of the location, character and ends of exegetical labour. In a theological culture in which exegetical self-understanding is often formed by other, less fruitful, influences, the development of a dogmatic account of Scripture may have a certain polemical timeliness. But what it may not do is replace or eclipse the work of exegesis.

An earlier version of the material was delivered at the University of Aberdeen in May 2001, as the *Scottish Journal of Theology* lectures. I am deeply grateful for the invitation to give the lectures, as well as to friends and colleagues in Aberdeen who took time to discuss their substance with me. And I am particularly indebted to Iain and Morag Torrance for their many kindnesses.

[2] Ibid., pp. 7f.

1 | Revelation, Sanctification and Inspiration

Holy Scripture is not a single or simple entity. The term 'Holy Scripture' refers primarily to a set of texts, but importantly and secondarily to its divine origin and its use by the church. Thus the content of the term can only be thoroughly mapped by seeing this set of texts in connection with purposive divine action in its interaction with an assemblage of creaturely events, communities, agents, practices and attitudes. To talk of the biblical writings as Holy Scripture is ultimately to refer to more (but not to less!) than those writings *per se*. It is, on the one hand, to depict these texts in the light of their origin, function and end in divine self-communication, and, on the other hand, to make recommendations about the kinds of responses to these texts which are fitting in view of their origin, function and end. 'Holy Scripture' is a shorthand term for the nature and function of the biblical writings in a set of communicative acts which stretch from God's merciful self-manifestation to the obedient hearing of the community of faith.

The sufficiency of Scripture, that is, is not quite the same as its 'self-sufficiency'.[1] Yet whilst 'Holy Scripture' does refer to a composite

---

[1] The distinction between 'sufficiency' and 'self-sufficiency' is drawn firmly by T. Ward in *Word and Supplement. Speech Acts, Biblical Texts, and the Sufficiency of Scripture* (Oxford: Oxford University Press, 2002), who seeks to clarify 'in theological and hermeneutical terms the senses in which "the sufficiency of Scripture" is necessarily a circumscribed concept'. Hence he criticises both the iconic theories of text in the 'New Criticism' and the highly formalist understanding of scripture in Hans Frei, which he terms 'hyper-sufficiency' (p. 150), and which confuses the objectivity of a text with its self-sufficiency (see p. 198). Ward's counter-suggestion is to appeal to Derrida's notion

reality (texts in relation to revelation and reception), there is a definite order to its elements. Most of all, both the texts and the processes surrounding their reception are subservient to the self-presentation of the triune God, of which the text is a servant and by which readers are accosted, as by a word of supreme dignity, legitimacy and effectiveness. This order is critically important because, unless their strict subservience to communicative divine activity is stated with some firmness, both text and practices of reading and reception may break loose and become matters for independent or quasi-independent investigation and explanation. When that is allowed to take place, the result is a disorderly ontology of Holy Scripture.

One type of disorder – the isolation of the text both from its place in God's revelatory activity and from its reception in the community of faith – has, as we shall see, long been a problem in Western divinity since the Reformation. A somewhat different kind of disorder results when the term 'Holy Scripture' is expounded in such a way that its primary (or sometimes exclusive) reference is to the uses of the biblical texts made by readers, and only secondarily (if at all) to the place of the texts in the economy of God's communicative grace. By way of example: in *What is Scripture?* Wilfred Cantwell Smith presents a sustained argument that 'Scriptures are not texts!'[2] – that the term

of textual 'supplements' and, most especially, to Wolterstorff's deployment of speech-act theory, which 'shows how authors, their texts and meanings, and readers, exist meaningfully only in that they are related to one another, without the otherness of any one element being subsumed into another' (pp. 198f.). Ward's ordering of the relation of divine action to the human activities of authorship and reading rightly prioritises the divine agent. Yet – almost inevitably in a work which invests a good deal in the conceptual resources afforded by a philosophical theory of communicative action – Ward's deployment of dogmatic materials is decidedly modest. One may legitimately wonder whether speech-act theory can furnish all that is required for a 'critical retrieval' of the classical Protestant doctrine of Scripture, and whether much more extensive appeal to such concepts as revelation and inspiration (and so, therefore, to the doctrine of the Trinity) is required.

[2] W. Cantwell Smith, *What is Scripture? A Comparative Approach* (London: SCM, 1993), p. 223. By contrast, T. Ward is entirely correct to insist on the need for an ontology of

'Scripture' is a way of talking about human practices vis-à-vis texts rather than about texts themselves:

> *There is no ontology of scripture.* The concept has no metaphysical, nor logical, referent; there is nothing that scripture finally 'is' . . . [A]t issue is not the texts of scripture that are to be understood and about which a theory is to be sought, but the dynamic of human involvement with them . . . Scripture has been . . . a human activity: it has been also a human propensity, a potentiality. There is no ontology of scripture; just as, at a lower level, there is no ontology of art, nor of language, nor of other things that we human beings do, and are. Rather than existing independently of us, all these are subsections of the ontology of our being persons.[3]

A much more theologically complex examination of the issues is offered by Ingolf Dalferth, who explores a distinction between the singular term 'Scripture' (*Schrift*) and the plural term 'scriptures' or 'writings' (*Schriften*). Where the latter refers to the biblical writings *per se*, the former refers to these writings in their use by the faith community. 'Scripture' is thus 'the use made of the scriptures of the Bible in . . . the event of the church's proclamation';[4] hence ingredient within the concept of 'Scripture' is 'the Christian *community* or church' which uses the biblical writings as Scripture.[5] Dalferth's concern is, clearly, a legitimate Reformation point of conscience: the desire to avoid any account of the nature of Scripture *extra usum*, and to insist on determining the nature of Scripture *in usu et actione*. The

Scripture, and on the need to root the use of the text in the properties of the text: *Word and Supplement*, pp. 300–2.

[3] Cantwell Smith, *What is Scripture?* p. 237.

[4] I. U. Dalferth, 'Die Mitte ist außen. Anmerkungen zum Wirklichkeitsbezug evangelischer Schriftauslegung', in C. Landmesser et al., eds., *Jesus Christus als die Mitte der Schrift. Studien zur Hermeneutik des Evangeliums* (Berlin: de Gruyter, 1997), p. 183.

[5] Ibid.; see also I. U. Dalferth, 'Von der Vieldeutigkeit der Schrift und der Eindeutigkeit des Wortes Gottes', in R. Ziegert, ed., *Die Zukunft des Schriftprinzips* (Stuttgart: Deutsche Bibelgesellschaft, 1994), p. 169.

difficulty arises when use and action are identified too closely with 'kerygmatic-doxological use' of Scripture by the church.[6] Dalferth certainly avoids Cantwell Smith's collapse of the notion of Scripture into that of community usage by insisting on the coinherence of Scripture, church and faith with communicative divine presence; but his claim that, nevertheless, the term 'Scripture' identifies an aspect of Christian *Lebenspraxis* without empirical content[7] points in a quite different direction, one in which the corporate subjectivity of the church looms very large.

What is required, and what this book tries to sketch, is a dogmatic account of the nature of Holy Scripture which neither restricts the scope of what the term indicates (texts in relation to God's communication and its hearing) nor allows the element of creaturely reception to become inflated. The first three chapters undertake such an account by looking at the relation of Scripture to the divine acts of revelation, sanctification and inspiration, and then at the churchly and readerly acts of receiving the Word of God. Crucially, my suggestion is that the proper connections between the various elements (revelation, text, community, faithful reception) can only be retained by their careful dogmatic specification.

This first chapter begins the task of mapping Christian talk of the Bible as Holy Scripture in a dogmatic projection by arguing that an essential task of the term 'Holy Scripture' is to indicate the place occupied by the biblical texts in the revealing, sanctifying and inspiring acts of the triune God. Holy Scripture is dogmatically explicated in terms of its role in God's self-communication, that is, the acts of Father, Son and Spirit which establish and maintain that saving fellowship with humankind in which God makes himself known to us and by us.[8] The 'sanctification' of Scripture (its 'holiness') and its 'inspiration' (its proceeding from God) are aspects of the process

---

[6] Dalferth, 'Von der Vieldeutigkeit', p. 163; cf. 'Die Mitte ist außen', p. 183.

[7] 'Die Mitte ist außen', p. 185.

[8] The rooting of the doctrine of Scripture in the doctrine of the triune God is consistently emphasised in A. Wenz, *Das Wort Gottes – Gericht und Rettung*.

whereby God employs creaturely reality in his service, for the attestation of his saving self-revelation. Thus, what is said about the sanctification and inspiration of Scripture is an extension of what is said about revelation; but what is said about revelation is an extension of what is said about the triune God. What Scripture is as sanctified and inspired is a function of divine revelatory activity, and divine revelatory activity is God's triune being in its external orientation, its gracious and self-bestowing turn to the creation.

The first task, then, is to offer an overall sketch of the doctrine of Holy Scripture by examining three primary concepts: revelation, sanctification and inspiration. The first and third terms are familiar in theological discussion of the nature of Scripture, and, although I argue that some careful dogmatic specification of these terms is required if they are to be serviceable, appeal to them should hold no surprises. However, the second term, 'sanctification', may seem somewhat out of place, since its more usual application is in discussion of soteriology, specifically in giving a theological account of the 'application' of salvation, that is, the effectiveness of Christ in the lives of believers. But although the primary field in which the term is deployed remains that of the relation between divine and human persons, it may legitimately be extended to non-personal realities in so far as they are instruments of the personal relations between God and humankind. 'Sanctification' is not improperly used in this way in, for example, sacramental theology, to indicate the segregation of creaturely realities by virtue of their moulding and use by God to undertake specific tasks in the economy of salvation. In this sense, a 'sanctified' reality is most generally described as set apart by God as a means of divine self-communication. In the context of discussing the relation between divine self-revelation and the nature of Holy Scripture, sanctification functions as a middle term, indicating in a general way God's activity of appointing and ordering the creaturely realities

Untersuchungen zur Autorität der Heiligen Schrift in Bekenntnis und Lehre der Kirche (Göttingen: Vandenhoeck und Ruprecht, 1996).

of the biblical texts towards the end of the divine self-manifestation. The scope of its application is thus wider than the term 'inspiration', which is best restricted to discussion of the more specific question of the relation between divine self-communicative acts and Scripture as textual entity. It is certainly true that, with declining confidence in the viability of a dogmatic notion of verbal inspiration, the range of the term 'inspiration' has in some modern theology been considerably broadened, to become equivalent to, for example, a supposed intuitive awareness of the divine on the part of the biblical authors, or the illumination of the readers of the biblical text. A more orderly account of the matter will, however, restrict the application of the term to the specific set of divine acts in respect of the production of the biblical texts, and look for a term of wider reach to indicate the overall process of God's ordering of creaturely realities as servants of his self-presentation. For this wider task, I suggest the adoption of the term 'sanctification'.

As used here, it is closely related to two other tracts of theological doctrine, namely providence and the theology of mediation. 'Providence' speaks of the divine activities of ordering creaturely realities to their ends; 'mediation' speaks of the instrumentality of created realities in the divine working. Both terms are readily applicable in the context of discussing the nature of Scripture. God's work of overseeing such processes as tradition-history, redaction, authorship and canonisation could well be described in terms of the divine providential acts of preserving, accompanying and ruling creaturely activities, annexing them to his self-revelation. And the function of these providentially ordered texts in the divine economy could be depicted as mediatorial. If the term 'sanctification' is still to be preferred, it is, as I hope to show, because it covers much of the same ground as both of these terms, whilst also addressing in a direct way the relation of divine activity to creaturely process, without sliding into dualism. But the terms are certainly porous, and in and of themselves they are of little consequence; all that matters is their fittingness for the task of orderly explication of the matter itself.

Revelation

Like many other stretches of Christian teaching, the Christian doctrine of revelation suffers from the distortions of its shape introduced by attempts to formulate and expound it in relation to and, in some measure, in dependence upon, dominant modern intellectual and spiritual conventions. Indeed, this *locus* of Christian theology is a particularly acute register of the distress felt by modern Christian theology when faced by the collapse of the cultural metaphysic in which classical Christianity had developed and which, indeed, it helped to form. As that overarching framework crumbled, Christian theological teaching about revelation became at one and the same time desperately unworkable and desperately necessary: unworkable, because of what was feared to be irrefutable philosophical and moral challenge; necessary, because any possible response to that challenge seemed ultimately to require a defence of Christian claims by a reconstruction of the possibility of revelation, a reconstruction in which the guiding hand was very often philosophical rather than dogmatic. Both the lack of viability and the urgent need for reconstruction are symptomatic, however, of the severe *doctrinal* disarray in which Christian teaching found itself in modernity. If the doctrine of revelation has stumbled and fallen, it has not only been because Christian theology was tongue-tied in trying to answer its critics to their satisfaction; it has also been because Christian theology found itself largely incapable of following and deploying the inner logic of Christian conviction in its apologetic and polemical undertakings. And the reason for that failure on the part of Christian theology is that theology itself had in important respects already lost touch with an orderly understanding of God's self-communication, and in its place offered rather stripped-down or misshapen versions of the topic. Most tellingly, these reduced accounts of revelation were seriously under-determined by the specifically Christian content of Christian teaching about God. 'Revelation', that is, was transposed rather readily into a feature of generally 'theistic' metaphysical outlooks. As such

11

it could be expounded generically, without much by way of concrete material reference to those aspects of the Christian apprehension about God which mark out its positivity: Christology, pneumatology, soteriology and – embracing them all – the doctrine of the Trinity. Understood in this dogmatically minimalistic way, language about revelation became a way of talking, not about the life-giving and loving presence of the God and Father of our Lord Jesus Christ in the Spirit's power among the worshipping and witnessing assembly, but instead of an arcane process of causality whereby persons acquire knowledge through opaque, non-natural operations. In short: failure to talk with much by way of Christian determinacy about revelation – whether on the part of its opponents or of its defenders – left the doctrine pitifully weak, and scarcely able to extricate itself from the web of objections in which it was entangled.

Yet at the very same time that the doctrine was eviscerated in this way, the demands placed upon it increased to a point where they became insupportable. Perhaps the most significant symptom of this is the way in which Christian theological talk of revelation migrates to the beginning of the dogmatic corpus, and has to take on the job of furnishing the epistemological warrants for Christian claims. This absorption of revelation into foundations has two effects. First, it promotes the hypertrophy of revelation by making it responsible for providing the platform on which all subsequent Christian teaching is erected; and thereby, second, it exacerbates the isolation of talk of revelation from the material dogmatic considerations (Trinity, incarnation, Spirit, church) through its mislocation and its reassignment to undertake duties which it was not intended to perform. This latter aspect of the fate of Christian teaching about revelation had particularly damaging consequences for Christian theological thinking about the nature of Scripture. For alongside the hypertrophy of revelation and its migration into epistemology, there develops a parallel process whereby revelation and Scripture are strictly identified. As this happens, then Scripture's role as the *principium cognoscendi* of Christian faith and theology comes to be thought of in such a way that Scripture precedes and warrants all other Christian doctrines as the formal principle from which those other doctrines are deduced.

If this unhappy process is to be countered, what is required is not more effective defence of the viability of Christian talk about revelation before the tribunal of impartial reason: the common doctrinal slenderness of such defences nearly always serves to inflame rather than reduce the dogmatic difficulties. The doctrinal underdetermination and mislocation of the idea of revelation can only be overcome by its reintegration into the comprehensive structure of Christian doctrine, and most especially the Christian doctrine of God. The most important consequence of this reintegration will be to call into question the idea that the doctrine of revelation is a tract of Christian teaching with quasi-independent status; this will in turn offer the possibility of an orderly exposition of revelation as a corollary of more primary Christian affirmations about the nature, purposes and saving presence of the triune God. Moreover, straightening out some of the disorder of the theology of revelation will release Christian teaching about Holy Scripture from some of the inhibitions under which it has operated, and so encourage a more fruitful exposition of that locus.

In thesis form, the argument to be set out here may be stated thus: *revelation is the self-presentation of the triune God, the free work of sovereign mercy in which God wills, establishes and perfects saving fellowship with himself in which humankind comes to know, love and fear him above all things.*

Revelation, first, is *the self-presentation of the triune God.* Revelation, that is, is a way of talking about those acts in which God makes himself present; indeed, '[r]evelation is . . . divine presence'.[9] This may be expanded in two directions.

---

[9] K. Barth, 'Revelation', in *God in Action* (Edinburgh: T. & T. Clark, 1936), p. 8; on the coinherence of revelation and divine presence, see again Ingolf Dalferth: 'Von der Vieldeutigkeit', 'Die Mitte ist außen', and, more generally, his essay 'Theologie und Gottes Gegenwart', in *Gedeutete Gegenwart. Zur Wahrnehmung Gottes in den*

First, the *content* of revelation is God's own proper reality. Revelation is not to be thought of as the communication of arcane information or hidden truths, as if in revelation God were lifting the veil on something other than his own self and indicating it to us. Talk of revelation is not talk of some reality separable from God's own being, something which God as it were deposits in the world and which then becomes manipulable. Revelation is divine *self*-presentation; its content is identical with God. To speak of revelation is simply to point to the divine self-utterance: I am who I am. '[R]evelation . . . is nothing less than God Himself.'[10]

Second, the *agent* of revelation is God himself: God presents himself. The realisation of the presence of God is not an undertaking of an agent other than God; God is not inert or inactive but eloquent, 'speaking out' of himself. Part of the force, indeed, of the use of the metaphor of speech in talking of divine revelation as 'God's Word' is to indicate that God is outgoing, communicative, antecedently one who comes to and addresses creaturely reality, making himself present as that which conditions and determines that reality in its entirety.

Revelation, therefore is identical with God's triune being in its active self-presence. As Father, God is the personal will or origin of this self-presence; as Son, God actualises his self-presence, upholding it and establishing it against all opposition; as Holy Spirit, God perfects that self-presence by making it real and effective to and in the history of humankind. To speak of 'revelation' is to say that God is one whose being is directed towards his creatures, and the goal of whose free self-movement is his presence with us.

Second, as God's free self-presentation, revelation is a *free work of sovereign mercy*. God's revelation is God's *spiritual* presence: God is the personal subject of the act of revelation, and therefore revelation

Erfahrungen der Zeit (Tübingen: Mohr, 1997), pp. 268–85; see also D. Ritschl's earlier study *Memory and Hope. An Inquiry into the Presence of Christ* (New York: Macmillan, 1967).

[10] Barth, 'Revelation', p. 12.

can in no way be commodified. God is – as Gérard Siegwalt puts it – revelation's 'uncontainable content'.[11] As spiritual presence, the presence of God is free; it is not called forth by any reality other than itself; it is majestically spontaneous and uncaused. Its origin, actualisation and accomplishment require nothing beyond God. Like the entire history of the divine mercy of which it is part, revelation is unexpected, undeserved, possible only as and because God is, and present after the manner of God. In Barth's curious phrase, 'God is the Lord in the wording of His Word.'[12]

This is why revelation is *mystery*, a making known of 'the mystery of God's will' (Eph. 1.9). That is to say, revelation is the manifest presence of God which can only be had on its own terms, and which cannot be converted into something plain and available for classification. Revelation is God's *presence*; but because it is *God's* presence, it is not direct and unambiguous openness such that henceforth God is plain. To think in such terms of an 'open and directly given revelation'[13] would be to historicise or naturalise God's personal revelatory activity, reducing it to an intra-mundane phenomenon – a danger which, as we shall see, has afflicted much Christian theological talk about the nature of Holy Scripture. 'The holy that is obvious, the sacral, is never the true holy. The true holy is spirit, not thing. The *Deus dixit* is revelation, not revealedness.'[14]

So far, then, revelation is God's self-presentation in free mercy. As this self-presentation, revelation is, third, the establishment of *saving fellowship*. Revelation is purposive. Its end is not simply divine self-display, but the overcoming of human opposition, alienation and

---

[11] G. Siegwalt, 'Le canon biblique et la révélation', in *Le christianisme, est-t-il une religion du livre?* (Strasbourg: Faculté de théologie protestante, 1984), p. 46.

[12] K. Barth, *Church Dogmatics* I/1 (Edinburgh: T. & T. Clark, 1975), p. 139. This more material account of revelation as the exercise of divine freedom is to be preferred to the rather formal explication of revelation out of the notion of divine prevenience offered by R. Thiemann in his otherwise helpful account *Revelation and Theology. The Gospel as Narrated Promise* (Notre Dame: Notre Dame University Press, 1985), e.g. pp. 6f., 9.

[13] K. Barth, *The Göttingen Dogmatics*, vol. 1 (Grand Rapids: Eerdmans, 1991), p. 59.

[14] Ibid.

pride, and their replacement by knowledge, love and fear of God. In short: revelation is reconciliation. 'This is what revelation means', writes Barth, 'this is its content and dynamic: Reconciliation has been made and accomplished. Reconciliation is not a truth which revelation makes known to us; reconciliation is the truth of God Himself who grants Himself freely to us in His revelation.'[15]

As the gracious presence of God, revelation is itself the establishment of fellowship. It is not so much an action in which God informs us of other acts of his through which we are reconciled to him; rather, revelation is a way of indicating the communicative force of God's saving, fellowship-creating presence. God is present as saviour, and so communicatively present. The notions of God as revealer and God as reconciler are sometimes thought to tug in different directions: 'revealer' suggests an excessively noetic understanding of our relation to God, and 'reconciler' corrects this by emphasising participation or communion in the life of God.[16] But the contrast is specious. For, on the one hand, fellowship with God is communicative fellowship in which God is known; it is not a mere unconscious ontological participation in God. And, on the other hand, knowledge of God in his revelation is no mere cognitive affair: it is to know *God* and therefore to love and fear the God who appoints us to fellowship with himself, and not merely to entertain God as a mental object, however exalted. Revelation is thus not simply the bridging of a noetic divide (though it includes that), but is reconciliation, salvation and therefore fellowship. The idiom of revelation is as much moral and relational as it is cognitional. Revelation is the self-giving presence of God which overthrows opposition to God, and, in reconciling, brings us into the light of the knowledge of God.

If we stand back a pace from this brief sketch of revelation as presence, grace and reconciliation, we notice particularly that the proper doctrinal location for talk of revelation is the Christian doctrine of

[15] Barth, 'Revelation', p. 17.

[16] Barth is the usual culprit; the most sensitive account of his crimes is A. Torrance, *Persons in Communion* (Edinburgh: T. & T. Clark, 1996).

the Trinity, and, in particular, the outgoing, communicative mercy of the triune God in the economy of salvation. Revelation is the corollary of trinitarian theology and soteriology. 'The centre is not divine self-identification but divine saving action. Thus it is preferable to say that revelation is first of all a function of that divine action by which the redemption of the creation is achieved in such a way that human blindness and ignorance are also removed. To that extent the doctrine of revelation should be understood as a function of the doctrine of salvation.'[17] What Christian theology has to say about revelation is not simply deployed as a means of dealing with epistemological questions, or primarily as an answer to questions of the sources and norms of church and theological discourse. It may address these concerns, but it does so as an application or extension of its material content, which is the sovereign goodness of Father, Son and Spirit in willing, realising and perfecting saving fellowship. 'Revelation' denotes the communicative, fellowship-establishing trajectory of the acts of God in the election, creation, providential ordering, reconciliation, judgement and glorification of God's creatures.

Sanctification

The argument so far can be summed up by saying that a Christian theology of revelation becomes dysfunctional when its bonds to the doctrine of the Trinity disintegrate; consequently, that rebuilding a doctrine of revelation is inseparable from attention to the properly Christian doctrine of God. From here, we turn to sketch in general terms the way in which the creaturely reality of Scripture serves in the saving economy of God's self-communication, by explicating the term 'sanctification'. In briefest form, sanctification is the act of God the Holy Spirit in hallowing creaturely processes, employing them in the service of the taking form of revelation within the history of

---

[17] C. Gunton, *A Brief Theology of Revelation* (Edinburgh: T. & T. Clark, 1995), p. 111.

the creation. As with revelation, so here: the doctrine of the Trinity proves itself to be of critical importance in giving an account of the relation of God's self-communication to the creaturely reality of the biblical text. For – to put the matter at its simplest – the tendency of modern intellectual culture to bifurcate the transcendent reality of God and the creaturely texts of the Bible can only be countered by appeal to a Christian doctrine of the trinitarian works of God. In particular, an account of the relation between revelation and the Bible needs to draw heavily upon the resources of the theology of the Spirit of the risen Christ as the free, active self-presence of the triune God in creation, sanctifying creaturely realities for the divine service and, more specifically, inspiring the biblical writings.

Such Christological-pneumatological considerations help prevent the theology of Scripture from being overwhelmed by a burden which has sorely afflicted the intellectual conscience of modern Western divinity (especially Protestant divinity), which continues to haunt us, and for which there has emerged no commonly agreed resolution. That burden is the question of how we are to conceive the relation between the biblical texts as so-called 'natural' or 'historical' entities and theological claims about the self-manifesting activity of God. The problems referred to here are neither single nor stable, and a full exposition of them would require very considerable historical delicacy. But the core of the problem may be indicated in the following rather rough terms.

Much modern study of the Bible has understood its task as that of the investigation of what early on in the development of critical scholarship Spinoza called 'the "history" of Scripture'.[18] That is, the job of the biblical scholar consists in inquiry into and interpretation of the text as a natural entity through the investigation of its language, provenance, authorship, reception and subsequent career.

---

[18] B. de Spinoza, *A Theologico-Political Treatise*, in *The Chief Works of Benedict de Spinoza*, vol. 1 (New York: Dover, 1951), p. 103.

Though some modern critical strategies of investigation may have greater sophistication than that of Spinoza (in, for example, analysing rhetorical, socio-economic or ideological aspects of the history of Scripture), the basic historical naturalism remains. Affirmations of the role played by the text in the revelatory economy of God are not considered germane to determining what the text is; if considerations of any such role are entertained, it is only after fundamental determinations of the substance of the text have been reached on historical grounds. For a Christian theological account of Scripture, the problem raised here is a matter not so much of what is affirmed but of what is denied. The problem, that is, is not the affirmation that the biblical texts have a 'natural history', but the denial that texts with a 'natural history' may function within the communicative divine economy, and that such a function is ontologically definitive of the text. It is this denial – rather than any purely methodological questions – which has to form the focus of dogmatic critique.[19]

Part of what lies behind this denial is the complex legacy of dualism and nominalism in Western Christian theology, through which the sensible and intelligible realms, history and eternity, were thrust

---

[19] This is not to overlook the important *political* aspects of the rise of historical interpretation of Scripture, emphasised by H. G. Reventlow in *The Authority of the Bible and the Rise of the Modern World* (London: SCM, 1980) and more fully by J. Samuel Preus in an important essay *Spinoza and the Irrelevance of Biblical Authority* (Cambridge: Cambridge University Press, 2001), where it is argued that one of the crucial ways in which Spinoza undermined the legitimating function of Scripture for theocratic government was by challenging the office of the authoritative public interpreter of Scripture: 'naturalizing' Scripture rendered redundant the claims of privileged interpreters to be able to make public law, and thereby contributed to the cause of liberty. Preus' handling of the dogmatic issues is less than secure; and one might question the underlying unambiguously positive evaluation of modern traditions of libertarian thought (the undifferentiated use of the term 'fundamentalist' to describe Spinoza's opponents – in his day and our own – gives the game away). Nevertheless, the centrality of the relationship of the exegetical and the political to an understanding of modernity is beyond dispute (and could be traced back at least as far as Bacon: see A. Grafton, *Defenders of the Text. The Traditions of Scholarship in an Age of Science, 1450–1800* (Cambridge, Mass.: Harvard University Press, 1991)).

away from each other, and creaturely forms (language, action, institutions) denied any capacity to indicate the presence and activity of the transcendent God. The ramifications are felt throughout the corpus of Christian teaching: in debates about justification, about the nature of the church, about divine grace and human free will, or about the nature of political society. But they are seen with special vividness in Christian teaching about the nature of the Bible, for at least three reasons: the prominence of Scripture as a norm in Protestant church life and theology; the particular construals of the inspiration of Scripture which emerged in post-Reformation confessional theology; and the extraordinary prestige which historical science acquired in the course of its application to canonical Christian texts. All these factors conspired to exacerbate the distress felt by Christian theology once critical history came to dominate its intellectual culture.

The problem, however, was not restricted to naturalistic biblical critics, for the dualistic framework of modern historical naturalism as applied to the study of the biblical texts was in many respects shared by those who resisted the claims of critical history. The disorder of Christian theological language about the Bible in modernity, that is, was further compounded by the way in which some theologians leapt to the defence of Scripture by espousing a strident supernaturalism, defending the relation of the Bible to divine revelation by almost entirely removing it from the sphere of historical contingency, through the elaboration of an increasingly formalised and doctrinally isolated theory of inspiration. Rather than deploying theological resources to demonstrate how creaturely entities may be the servants of the divine self-presence, they sought to dissolve the problem by as good as eliminating one of its terms: the creatureliness of the text. From one angle, the result is docetic – a text without any kind of home in natural history. From another angle, the result is ironically historicising, a de-eschatologizing of the text's relation to revelation by envisaging the text as an apparently creaturely object endowed with divine properties.

Both naturalism and supernaturalism are trapped, however, in a competitive understanding of the transcendent and the historical. Either the naturalness of the text is safeguarded by extracting it from any role in God's self-communication, or the relation of the text to revelation is affirmed by removing the text from the historical conditions of its production. Pure naturalism and pure supernaturalism are mirror images of each other; and both are fatally flawed by the lack of a thoroughly theological ontology of the biblical texts.

The plunge into dualism is inseparable from the retrenchment of the doctrine of Trinity in theological talk of God's relation to the world. When God's action towards the world is conceived in a non-trinitarian fashion, and, in particular, when Christian talk of the presence of the risen Christ and the activity of the Holy Spirit does not inform conceptions of divine action in the world, then that action comes to be understood as external, interruptive, and bearing no real relations to creaturely realities. God, in effect, becomes causal will, intervening in creaturely reality from outside but unconnected to the creation. This frankly dualistic framework can only be broken by replacing the monistic and monergistic idea of divine causality with an understanding of God's continuing free presence and relation to the creation through the risen Son in the Spirit's power. In this continuing relation, creaturely activities and products can be made to serve the saving self-presentation of God without forfeiting their creaturely substance, and without compromise to the eschatological freedom of God.

It is precisely here that the notion of sanctification proves its utility. For the notion of Scripture as 'sanctified' addresses the cluster of problems we have been reviewing by offering a dogmatic ontology of the biblical texts which elides neither their creatureliness nor their relation to the free self-communication of God. At its most basic, the notion states that the biblical texts are creaturely realities set apart by the triune God to serve his self-presence. Thereby, talk of sanctification moves discussion of the nature of Scripture out of the dualisms of what Gordon Spykman calls 'two-factor theologies',[20] which continue to force a choice between either a divine or a human text, either inspiration or naturalism.

Before moving to explore the notion of sanctification in more detail, however, it is important to review a number of different terms which might be deployed to state the relation of a creaturely text to divine revelation. Five terms are of particular significance.

First, a long tradition of Protestant dogmatics appealed to the notion of the divine act of accommodation or condescension in the use of human language and texts for the communication of divine verities. However, as expounded in Protestant scholasticism, the notion of accommodation is tied to an excessively neat distinction between, on the one hand, the form, manner or mode of revelation and, on the other hand, the content of revelation. The first (form) is associated with the human character of the biblical texts, the second (content) with the matter of divine wisdom to which this form is external. Although accommodation and (especially) condescension give proper emphasis to the way in which the biblical texts are what they are in the economy of God's self-revelation, the distinction between form and content can have the effect of inflaming the problem of dualism by reinforcing the idea that the creatureliness of the text is simply external and contingent.

A related difficulty arises with the use of the analogy of the hypostatic union to conceptualise the relation of the divine and human elements in Scripture: in the same way that divine and human natures are united in the incarnate Word, so in the scriptural word divine and human are brought together without confusion and without separation. Like any extension of the notion of incarnation (in ecclesiology or ethics, for example) the result can be Christologically disastrous, in that it may threaten the uniqueness of the Word's becoming flesh

[20] G. Spykman, *Reformational Theology. A New Paradigm for Doing Dogmatics* (Grand Rapids: Eerdmans, 1992), p. 122.

by making 'incarnation' a general principle or characteristic of divine action in, through or under creaturely reality. But the Word made flesh and the scriptural word are in no way equivalent realities. Moreover, the application of an analogy from the hypostatic union can scarcely avoid divinising the Bible by claiming some sort of ontological identity between the biblical texts and the self-communication of God. Over against this, it has to be asserted that no divine nature or properties are to be predicated of Scripture; its substance is that of a creaturely reality (even if it is a creaturely reality annexed to the self-presentation of God); and its relation to God is instrumental. In the case of the Bible, there can be no question of 'a union of divine and human factors', but only of 'the mystery of the human words as God's Word'.[21]

Much less likely to beguile us into such problems is a third concept, namely that of Scripture as prophetic and apostolic testimony, much used by Barth throughout his writings, but found elsewhere in Reformed theology. What makes this a particularly helpful term is the way in which it retains the human character of the biblical materials without neglect of their reference to the Word and work of God. The very genre of 'testimony' – as language which attests a reality other than itself – is especially fitting for depicting how a creaturely entity may undertake a function in the divine economy, without resort to concepts which threaten to divinise the text, since – like prophecy or apostolic witness – testimony is not about itself but is a reference beyond itself. However, some careful specification is

---

[21] G. C. Berkouwer, *Holy Scripture* (Grand Rapids: Eerdmans, 1975), p. 203. J. de Senarclens, who makes much use of the analogy from the hypostatic union in his account of the nature of Scripture in *Heirs of the Reformation*, avoids the problems associated with this strategy by a strongly actualist insistence on the 'event' character of the relation of Scripture's humanity to its 'holiness'; yet it is at just this point that the analogy with the incarnation breaks down, for if this stress on event were transferred into the ontology of the person of Christ, the result would almost certainly be adoptionist. Further in criticism of the analogy, see L. Ayres and S. E. Fowl, '(Mis)reading the Face of God: *The Interpretation of the Bible in the Church*', *Theological Studies* 60 (1999), pp. 513–28.

needed, because the notion of Scripture as human testimony to God's revealing activity can suggest a somewhat accidental relation between the text and revelation. This is especially the case when the essential unsuitability or creaturely fragility of the testimony is so stressed (in order to protect the purity of the divine Word) that there appears to be little intrinsic relation between the texts and the revelation to which they witness. In this way, the annexation of the Bible to revelation can appear almost arbitrary: the text is considered a complete and purely natural entity taken up into the self-communication of God. The result is a curious textual equivalent of adoptionism. If the difficulty is to be retarded, however, it has to be by careful dogmatic depiction of the wider scope of the relation between God and the text, most of all by offering a theological description of the activity of God the Holy Spirit in sanctifying all the processes of the text's production, preservation and interpretation. Thereby the rather slender account of divine action vis-à-vis the text is filled out, without falling into the problems of undermining the creatureliness of the text which afflict talk of accommodation or the analogy of the hypostatic union.

Some of the same strengths are found in a fourth concept, that of Scripture as a 'means of grace'. The advantage of this concept is its soteriological idiom, its exposition of the nature of Scripture in terms of Scripture's place in the saving dealings of God with humankind, rather than simply as authority or epistemological norm.[22] Much hangs, however, on the way in which 'means' is understood. Like the

---

[22] For a recent strong defence of the notion of 'means of grace' as the primary theological category for talking of the nature of Scripture, see W. J. Abraham, *Canon and Criterion in Christian Theology. From the Fathers to Feminism* (Oxford: Clarendon Press, 1998). Some problems remain in Abraham's account, both historical (at a number of points his narrative of the place of Scripture in theology is open to serious challenge) and dogmatic (his assertion that Scripture is only one of a range of 'means of grace', and his consequent difficulties with making much sense of the notion of *sola scriptura*). See my essay 'Canon and Criterion: Some Reflections on a Recent Proposal', *Scottish Journal of Theology* 54 (2001), pp. 67–83.

notion of Scripture as testimony, it affords a way of affirming the instrumental role of Scripture in God's self-communication without rendering the means divine in itself. However, there is a tendency in any theology of mediation (sacramental, ministerial and symbolic as well as textual) to allow the mediating reality to eclipse the self-mediation of God in Christ and Spirit. Any notion of 'means', that is, has to be purged of the assumption that the mediated divine reality is itself inert or absent until 'presented' by that which mediates. Here the notion of testimony has some advantages, in that it conceives of Scripture as a reference to the active presence of another communicative agent rather than as an intermediary, bridging the gap between divine reality and human historical experience. Once again: Christology and pneumatology are crucial to orderly dogmatic exposition.

A final concept, very close in many respects to that of 'sanctification', is that of the 'servant-form' of Scripture, developed by Berkouwer in his fine study *Holy Scripture*, but owing much to his forbear Herman Bavinck. Throughout his book, Berkouwer argues against an unwarranted transcendentalism in talk of divine revelation, which, he argues, 'cannot be viewed as merely touching the circle of our reality and leaving it immediately thereafter'.[23] Rather, revelation – God's active presence as Word – is to be understood as 'treasure in earthen vessels' (2 Cor. 5.7), Scripture being the fitting creaturely servant of the divine act. 'The Word of God, Scripture in the form of a servant, is not known to us in the outlines of a supernatural miracle lifted out of time and human weakness . . . but in the human form of word and writing.'[24] The advantage of the concept of Scripture as servant is its affirmation that the creatureliness of the text is not an inhibition of its role in the communicative self-presentation of God; and so the text does not have to assume divine properties as a protection against contingency.

---

[23] Berkouwer, *Holy Scripture*, p. 195.   [24] Ibid., p. 207.

To draw the threads together: although the notion of 'accommodation' and the analogy from the hypostatic union may find it difficult to offer an account of the relation of creaturely texts to divine revelation without falling into transcendentalism, the notions of 'testimony', 'means of grace' and the 'servant-character' of Scripture are all resources to resist the drift into dualism. Here, however, we choose to make particular use of the conception of the text as a 'sanctified' reality, largely because, applied to the biblical texts, the concept of sanctification has greater range. Where notions like testimony, means of grace and service tend to apply most naturally to the text as finished entity, sanctification can more readily be applied to the full range of processes in which the text is caught up from pre-textual tradition to interpretation, thus reserving the term 'inspiration' to describe the specifically *textual* aspects of Scripture's service in the economy of grace.

In its broadest sense, sanctification refers to the work of the Spirit of Christ through which creaturely realities are elected, shaped and preserved to undertake a role in the economy of salvation: creaturely realities are sanctified by divine use. But it is important to emphasise that the divine 'use', though utterly gratuitous, is not simply occasional or punctiliar, an act from above which arrests and overwhelms the creaturely reality, employs it, and then puts it to one side. The sanctity of creaturely realities is certainly unthinkable without reference to the event of sanctification, for the creature's holiness is God's 'living work, the fruit of his intervention and the effect of his presence . . . the event of his coming, the personal and decisive gesture corresponding to his love and freedom'.[25] But precisely in its free transcendence of that which it employs in its service, divine use has a properly 'horizontal' dimension as well as a sheerly 'vertical' dimension. There is an election and overseeing of the entire historical course of the creaturely reality so that it becomes a creature which may serve the purposes of God. Sanctification is thus not the

---

[25] J. de Senarclens, *Heirs of the Reformation* (London: SCM, 1963), p. 276.

extraction of creaturely reality from its creatureliness, but the annexing and ordering of its course so that it may fittingly assist in that work which is proper to God.

Ingredient within the idea of sanctification is thus an understanding of God which is neither deist nor dualist. As the Holy Spirit's work, sanctification is a process in which, in the limitless freedom of God, the creaturely element is given its own genuine reality as it is commanded and moulded to enter into the divine service. God the sanctifying Spirit is both Lord and Life-giver. The sanctifying Spirit is *Lord*; that is, sanctification is not in any straightforward sense a process of cooperation or coordination between God and the creature, a drawing out or building upon some inherent holiness of the creature's own. Sanctification is *making* holy. Holiness is properly an incommunicable divine attribute; if creaturely realities become holy, it is by virtue of election, that is, by a sovereign act of segregation or separation by the Spirit as Lord. In this sense, therefore, the *sanctitas* of *sancta scriptura* is *aliena*. But the Spirit is *Life-giver*, the bestower of genuine and inalienable creaturely substance. From the vertical of 'lordship' there flows the horizontal of life which is truly *given*. Segregation, election to holiness, is not the abolition of creatureliness but its creation and preservation. In this sense, the *sanctitas* of *sancta scriptura* is *infusa*.

How does this notion of sanctification find particular application to the nature and function of the biblical texts in the economy of grace? As the work of the Spirit, sanctification integrates communicative divine action and the creatureliness of those elements which are appointed to the service of God's self-presentation. Talk of the biblical texts as *Holy* Scripture thus indicates a two-fold conviction about their place in divine revelation. First, because they are sanctified, the texts are not simply 'natural' entities, to be defined and interpreted exhaustively as such. They are fields of the Spirit's activity in the publication of the knowledge of God. Second, because sanctification does not diminish creatureliness, the texts' place in the divine economy does not entail their withdrawal from the realm of human processes. It is *as* – not *despite* – the creaturely realities that they are that they serve God.[26]

So used, the language of sanctification may help shake theology free from some of those sorry dualisms in which talk of Scripture has become enmeshed. A sanctified text is creaturely, not divine. Scripture's place in the economy of saving grace does not need to be secured by its divinisation through the unambiguous ascription of divine properties to the text. But as creaturely, the text is not thereby less serviceable, precisely because *as creature* it is sanctified (set apart, fashioned and maintained) for God's service. Crucially, 'creatureliness' is not to be confused with 'naturalness'. The latter concept is easily caught within the antithesis of nature and supernature; the former (pneumatological) concept allows that the creature (in this case, the text) can be a means of divine action without cost to its own substance. As sanctified creature, the text is not a quasi-divine artefact: sanctification is not transubstantiation. Nor is it an exclusively natural product arbitrarily commandeered by a supernatural agent. Sanctification is the Spirit's act of ordering creaturely history and being to the end of acting as *ancilla Domini*.

On this basis, what may be said of the ontology of the text? In its ordering by the Spirit's sanctifying work, the text has its being; its ontology is defined out of the formative economy of the Spirit of God. If this is difficult for us to grasp, it is because of a convention which so often presents itself to us as self-evidently authoritative, namely the convention that all texts are simply natural, historical entities, and that the Bible is to be read 'like any other text' because it *is* a text, and all texts are fundamentally the same kind of entity. But a general theory of texts has shown itself to have only scant theological utility. Such theory customarily determines what texts are in general and moves on from there to apply the resulting definitions and rules to specific

---

[26] Cf. the proposal of A. Wenz (*Das Wort Gottes*, p. 303) that 'God's speech and action occurs in, with and under creaturely means and historical processes – yet always in such a way that it takes place as speech and action which is strange, other, coming to the world and humankind from outside.'

texts. Thus Werner Jeanrond's *Text and Interpretation as Categories of Theological Thinking*[27] – surely a most sophisticated example of this argument – proposes to inquire into 'the textuality of texts'[28] as part of the 'development of a theory of understanding of texts in order to ground theological text interpretation in an appropriate foundational theory'.[29] What is problematic about this strategy is not only the foundationalism which inevitably accompanies assertions of the 'transcendental status of the theory of interpretation'.[30] There is a deeper, ontological, problem: the assumption that a text's being is defined by reference to its occupation of a space in a natural field of communicative activity. Both modern critical biblical scholarship and modern philosophical-theological hermeneutics are largely predicated on such a naturalist ontological assumption. Yet it is just the assumption that the biblical writings are instances of the natural class of texts which is to be resisted. Hermeneutically, it is a ruinous, even ludicrous, assumption, because it leads to the absurdity of developing a sophisticated critical apparatus to read biblical texts, not as what they are (texts which address the hearer in the name of God) but simply as textual clues in the business of reconstructing the matrices from which they emerged. Dogmatically, the assumption is to be controverted because of its claim that a 'natural' understanding of the text is more basic than an understanding of the text as 'scriptural'. In sum: the biblical text *is* Scripture; its being is defined, not simply by its membership of the class of texts, but by the fact that it is *this* text – sanctified, that is, Spirit-generated and preserved – in *this* field of action – the communicative economy of God's merciful friendship with his lost creatures.

Sanctification is not to be restricted to the text as finished product; it may legitimately be extended to the larger field of agents and actions of which the text is part. The Spirit's relation to the text broadens out into the Spirit's activity in the life of the people of God

---

[27] W. Jeanrond, *Text and Interpretation as Categories of Theological Thinking* (Dublin: Gill and Macmillan, 1988).
[28] Ibid., p. xvi.   [29] Ibid., pp. xvif.   [30] Ibid., p. xvii.

which forms the environment within which the text takes shape and serves the divine self-presence. Sanctification can thus properly be extended to the processes of the production of the text – not simply authorship (as, so often, in older theories of inspiration) but also the complex histories of pre-literary and literary tradition, redaction and compilation. It will, likewise, be extended to the post-history of the text, most particularly to canonisation (understood as the church's Spirit-produced acknowledgement of the testimony of Scripture) and to interpretation (understood as Spirit-illumined repentant and faithful attention to the presence of God). Westcott once wrote in connection with the process of canonisation of Scripture that 'we cannot understand the history of Christianity unless we recognise the action of the Holy Spirit in the Christian Society',[31] and his point – that a theological account of Scripture requires a pneumatological reading of the entire expanse of the life and acts of God's people – is of fundamental importance to our theme. This does not, of course, mean that the history of the processes surrounding the pre- and post-history of the biblical writings is to be reduced to an 'inert conduit',[32] any more than inspiration can be reduced to puppetry. Once again, the rule is: sanctification *establishes* and does not abolish creatureliness.

With this in mind, we turn to look in more detail at the notion of the inspiration of Scripture.

Inspiration

Inspiration is the specific textual application of the broader notion of sanctification as the hallowing of creaturely realities to serve revelation's taking form. Where sanctification indicates the dogmatic

---

[31] B. F. Westcott, *A General Survey of the History of the Canon of the New Testament* (Cambridge: Macmillan, 1881), p. xliv.

[32] B. Childs, 'On Reclaiming the Bible for Christian Theology', in C. Braaten and R. Jenson, eds., *Reclaiming the Bible for the Church* (Grand Rapids: Eerdmans, 1995), p. 9.

ontology of the text as the servant of the divine self-communicative presence, inspiration indicates the specific work of the Spirit of Christ with respect to the text. However, like the notion of revelation, that of inspiration is easily caught in some conceptual snares if it is displaced from its proper dogmatic location. The crucial task, therefore, is to 'clarify the logic of the term "inspire" as predicated of God'.[33] Such clarification, of course, is not merely conceptual; it is primarily dogmatic, that is, an orderly and well-proportioned arrangement of the thought and speech of the church in deference to the self-ordering truth of the gospel. Three particular requirements must be met if an account of inspiration is to be dogmatically profitable.

First, theological talk of the inspiration of Scripture needs to be strictly subordinate to and dependent upon the broader concept of revelation. Disorder threatens a theology of Scripture if the notion of inspiration is allowed to aggrandise itself and usurp the central place in bibliology. The disorder creeps in when the precise mode of Scripture's production and, most of all, the role played by the Holy Spirit in the inscripturation of revelation become the hinges on which all else turns. On such an account of the matter, inspiration is not an extrapolation from revelation and its taking form; on the contrary, it is foundational: Scripture is revelatory because it is inspired. The precise historical point at which this disorder begins to appear – whether in European Protestantism at the beginning of the seventeenth century, or in nineteenth-century American Reformed theology – is not at issue here. Whatever the genesis of the disorder, its effect is to warp the dogmatic framework of the theology of Scripture, as revelatory divine action is dislodged from its proper primacy, its place assumed by a particular construal of the Spirit's work in generating the biblical text. As Heppe puts it (he is criticising the Reformed scholastics, but what he says has wide application): on this model, 'the "divineness" of Scripture [is] derived purely – not

---

[33] W. J. Abraham, *The Divine Inspiration of Holy Scripture* (Oxford: Oxford University Press, 1981), p. 57.

from the participation of its authors in the facts of revelation and God's saving activity, but from the manner of its recording'.[34]

Properly understood, however, inspiration is not foundational but derivative, a corollary of the self-presence of God which takes form through the providential ordering and sanctification of creaturely auxiliaries. Talk of biblical inspiration follows from the fact that through Holy Scripture God addresses the church with the gospel of salvation. To reverse this direction, by arguing that the church knows that what Scripture declares is a word of salvation because Scripture is inspired, is to allow the pressure of the need for epistemological reassurance to distort the whole. Indeed, it is to make inspiration into a formal property insufficiently coordinated to the gospel content of Scripture, and to render the communicative presence of God contingent upon proven conviction of the text's inspiredness. In Calvin's 1542 *Antidote* to the Paris Articles, the matter is handled quite differently: 'since certainty of faith should be sought from none but God only', he says, 'we conclude that true faith is founded only on the Scriptures which proceeded from him, since therein he has been pleased to teach not partially, but fully, whatever he would have us know, and knew to be useful'.[35] Faith's certainty is grounded in God alone, not in inspiration; faith is 'founded' on Scripture, not because of its formal property as inspired but because Scripture is the instrument of divine teaching which proceeds from God. Within such a context, talk of inspiration will have its place; detached from that context, it goes awry.[36]

---

[34] H. Heppe, *Reformed Dogmatics* (London: George Allen and Unwin, 1950), p. 18.

[35] J. Calvin, *Articles Agreed Upon by the Faculty of Sacred Theology of Paris, with the Antidote* in *Tracts and Treatises*, vol. 1 (Edinburgh: Oliver and Boyd, 1958), p. 106.

[36] From this point of view, one of the major difficulties in David Law's recent study *Inspiration* (London: Continuum, 2001) is the way in which an account of inspiration is developed in what is primarily an apologetic context; theological language about inspiration attempts to provide a justification of the believer's acceptance of Scripture as authoritative (see, for example, p. 34, n. 68). The result is a curiously existentialist reworking of a common strategy amongst baroque Protestant theologians, namely the deployment of the doctrine of inspiration to furnish the epistemological grounds for

Second, consequently, the notion of inspiration needs to be expounded in a way which avoids both objectifying and spiritualising this divine activity.

Objectification happens when biblical inspiration is expounded in such a way that it makes revelation available after the manner of a worldly entity and not after the manner of God. In an objectified account of revelation, the inspired *product* is given priority over the revelatory, sanctifying and inspiring activities of the divine agent. But properly understood, inspiration does not mean that the truth of the gospel which Scripture sets before us becomes something to hand, constantly available independent of the Word and work of God, an entity which *embodies* rather than *serves* the presence of God. Inspiration does not spell the end of the mystery of God; it is simply that act of the Spirit through which this set of texts proceeds from God to attest his ineffable presence. Inspiration is a mode of the Spirit's freedom, not its inhibition by the letter. Once again, pressure to move in a different direction often comes from epistemological concerns – from the need to secure Scripture's foundational status as *inconcussum fundamentum veritatis* and *principium cognoscendi* by reference to inspiration. In effect, inspiration can become 'the purest form of epistemological apocalyptic',[37] knowledge without eschatology; and this dogmatics must eschew.

Spiritualisation of the notion of inspiration avoids objectification by shifting the centre of gravity away from the text and towards the persons associated with the text, whether authors or readers. Thus the nineteenth-century Danish bishop Martensen expounds the inspiration of Scripture as a function of 'the inspiration of the

---

the acceptance of Scripture's normative status, to describe, in other words, 'the processes by which the believer arrives at acceptance of biblical authority' (p. 35). Behind such a strategy lies a further difficulty, namely the inflammation of the notion of biblical *authority* into the primary dogmatic concept in bibliology, taking precedence even over such concepts as revelation or Word of God.

[37] G. Fackre, *The Doctrine of Revelation. A Narrative Interpretation* (Edinburgh: Edinburgh University Press, 1997), p. 170.

apostles' or 'apostolic consciousness';[38] it is not so much the case that Scripture is inspired but that it is 'the *ripened fruit* of inspiration'.[39] Or again, John Macquarrie proposes an account of the inspiration of Scripture which associates it with the community's reception of the text rather than with the text itself: 'Inspiration' is a way of talking of the 'power of bringing again or re-presenting the disclosure of the primordial revelation so that it speaks to us in our present experience', and as such 'does not lie in the words (it is not "verbal inspiration"), but belongs to the scriptures only as they are set in the context of the whole life of faith in the community'.[40] More recently, David Law has constructed an account of inspiration oriented not to the biblical text *per se* but to its readers. '"Inspiration" . . . does not describe a specific feature of the text but indicates rather how the reader should handle the Bible. It articulates the insight that the appropriate relation to the Bible on the part of the human being is submission to the Word of God which the Bible mediates.'[41] Thus 'the reader's role in the construction of textual meaning in reading the Bible entails the return of the concept of inspiration, but now inspiration is situated primarily in the *reader*'.[42] In effect, the term 'inspiration' gives a fairly light theological gloss to the subjective dispositions of the reader, eschewing any 'objective approach to the question of inspiration', which the book judges on other grounds to be an 'impossibility'.[43]

There are a number of dogmatic difficulties in such accounts. There is inevitably an immanentist cast in the notion of inspiration when we 'take the *reader's* relationship to the biblical writings as the starting-point for the construction of a theology of

[38] H. Martensen, *Christian Dogmatics* (Edinburgh: T. & T. Clark, 1898), p. 402.

[39] Ibid.

[40] J. Macquarrie, *Principles of Christian Theology* (London: SCM, 1966), p. 8.

[41] Law, *Inspiration*, p. 140.

[42] Ibid., p. 50. Law is drawing on U. H. J. Körtner, *Der inspirierter Leser. Zentrale Aspekte biblischer Hermeneutik* (Göttingen: Vandenhoeck und Ruprecht, 1994).

[43] Law, *Inspiration*, p. 143.

inspiration'[44] (though at least in Martensen's case the notion of 'apostolic consciousness' is backed up by a quite vigorously operative pneumatology[45]). But there is also, more seriously, a certain docetism in such accounts: the danger of objectification is countered by limiting the sphere of the Spirit's work to the psychic life of the apostles (Martensen), the community (Macquarrie) or the reader (Law) in such a way that the text itself is not touched by the inspiring action of God. And underlying both problems is a third, namely a reticence about talking of divine action through the textual service of Scripture, a sense of what Law calls the 'elusiveness' and 'inaccessibility' of the divine author.[46] As so often in the modern history of Scripture and its interpretation, the gap left by the withdrawal of the self-communicative divine presence is filled by readerly activity.

Both objectification and spiritualisation tend to repeat the dualism which the notion of sanctification was intended to eliminate; both, moreover, are pneumatologically deficient, whether by identifying the Spirit's relation to the text as a textual property *tout court*, or by excessive separation of Spirit and text. A more orderly model account of inspiration will thus refuse to identify inspiration either with textual properties or with the experience of author, community or reader, and instead give an account of inspiration which is primarily concerned with the communicative function of texts in the field of God's spiritual self-presence.

Third, the theological notion of inspiration needs to be expounded in clear connection to the end or purpose of Holy Scripture, which is service to God's self-manifestation. Like some kinds of crude cultic sacramental realism (of which it is a close cousin), a crass notion of verbal inspiration can abstract creaturely reality from its soteriological context, and so break its coinherence with Word, Spirit and faith. When this is allowed to happen, the scriptural word – like the sacramental element in isolation – becomes the Word, the

[44] Ibid., p. 144.   [45] Martensen, *Christian Dogmatics*, pp. 338–44.
[46] Law, *Inspiration*, p. 151.

Word made text, formalised, decontextualised and so dogmatically displaced. The pressures of polemic loom large in this process. Once the location of theological talk of the inspiration of Scripture shifts from *sacra doctrina* to foundations, and the purpose of such talk is the establishment of an inerrant doctrinal source and norm, then inspiration can be construed merely as a warrant for Scripture's *theological* authority, and therefore for its role in controversy. This process, of course, is an aspect of the larger historical shift of theology and theological thinking about the nature of the Bible away from practical-soteriological concerns to theoretical-polemical matters, a shift whose reverberations are felt throughout the corpus of Christian dogmatics but which has especially egregious effects in discussion of Scripture which, once again, orderly dogmatics must avoid.

With these three preliminaries in mind, we move to a more positive account of the nature of inspiration by way of commenting on one of the basic New Testament statements on the matter: 'Those moved by the Holy Spirit spoke from God' (2 Pet. 1.21). Four things may be said by way of conceptual paraphrase.

First, the leading theme of any account of inspiration must be ἀπο Θεοῦ (from God): inspiration is not primarily a textual property but a divine movement and therefore a divine moving. In any theologically adequate account of inspiration, therefore, the element of ἀπὸ Θεοῦ must be *operative* and *non-convertible*. It must be operative in the sense that language about the purpose and activity of God is not simply kept in the background, indicating a remote causal process with no present or immediate effectiveness. Accounts of scriptural inspiration are not infrequently curiously deistic, in so far as the biblical text can itself become a revelatory agent by virtue of an act of divine inspiration in the past. Thereby, however, ἀπὸ Θεοῦ is converted into a material condition; the 'movement' is arrested, objectified and commodified. But to talk of inspiration is not to suspend language of divine self-presentation but to trace one of its extensions into the creaturely realm.

Second, this 'from God' carries with it a negation: 'no prophecy ever came by the human will' (οὐ . . . θελήματι ἀνθρώπου). Talk of inspiration indicates that the generative impulse of the biblical text is not human spontaneity. Scripture *as text* is not in any fundamental sense a fruit of human poetics; its relation to human willing (here, that is, to literary creativity) is of a quite different order. This is because the domain in which the text has its rise is not that of the religious genius, but that of 'the power and coming of our Lord Jesus Christ' (2 Pet. 1.16). This coming, in its self-unfolding majesty, means that attestation of the divine glory is not a matter of 'cleverly devised myths' (verse 16); it is not a voluntary, self-originating movement, but a 'being moved'.

Third, this 'being moved' is particularly appropriated to the Holy Spirit. Language about the Spirit extends talk of God into the creaturely realm, in two ways. It ensures that creaturely objects and causes are indeed *moved* realities; their creaturely movement is not such that they are closed off from God, for that would be to deny the basic character of the gospel as a *divine* coming (παρουσία, verse 16). And it ensures that the divine coming is not purely transcendent; language about the Spirit is equally a protest against the secularisation of prophecy and the elimination of creatureliness.

Fourth, the Spirit generates language. Though what is said in this section of 2 Peter about scripture (γραφή) is said in relation to the more primary concern with prophecy (προφητεία), its applicability is evident: the moving of the Spirit, the direction of the ἀπὸ Θεοῦ, is to human communicative acts. Those moved by the Spirit *spoke*.

Here we reach the *particula veri* of the notion of *verbal* inspiration. Because verbal inspiration was routinely misconstrued (sometimes by its defenders and nearly always by its detractors) as entailing divine dictation, the notion of inspiration has been 'personalised' or 'de-verbalised' and redefined as authorial illumination. This distancing of inspiration from the verbal character of the text is considered to ease the difficulties of offering an account of inspiration by thinking of the words of the text as a purely human arena of activity, whether of authors, redactors or tradents. But the result is, again, docetic. The implied distinction between (inspired) content and (creaturely) form is awkward, and very easily makes authorial (or perhaps community) consciousness or experience the real substance of the text, of which words are external expressions. This is uncomfortably close to those styles of eucharistic theology in which the sacrament is considered to be a transaction between the gospel and the religious consciousness, to which visible forms are accidentally attached. No less than consecration, inspiration concerns the relation of God's communication and specific creaturely forms; inspiration, that is, involves *words*.

How, then, are we to understand what the older Protestant divines termed the *mandatum scribendi* or *impulsum scribendi*, the command or impulse to write? The relation of the words of Scripture to the communicative self-presence of God is not merely contingent; what revelation impels is writing. And because, therefore, we may not consider the words of Scripture as a purely natural product, it is proper to speak of the Spirit's impulse as involving the *suggestio verborum*. What is inspired is not simply the *matter* (*res*) of Scripture but its verbal *form* (*forma*). However, suggestion, mandate, impulse are acts of the Holy Spirit of the risen Jesus who is present to his creatures; they are not the causal working of a mute and remote power. The acts of the Spirit of the risen Christ entail no suspension of creatureliness. The prophets and apostles are not 'mere passive agents, mentally and volitionally inactive, and serving the Holy Spirit as a sort of speaking-tube . . . [A]lthough the prophets were moved, or driven, by the Holy Spirit, they *themselves* also spoke . . . their own activity was not suppressed by the moving of the Spirit but is lifted up, energized and purged'.[47] Being 'moved' by the Spirit is not simply being passively impelled; the Spirit's *suggestio* and human authorship are directly, not inversely, proportional; the action of the inspiring Spirit and the work of the inspired creature are concursive

---

[47] H. Bavinck, *Our Reasonable Faith* (Grand Rapids: Eerdmans, 1956), p. 102.

rather than antithetical. What is problematic about the language of dictation, or of the biblical writers as amanuenses of the Spirit, is not only that such notions make the text unrecognisable as a human historical product, but that they trade upon a confusion of God's omnicausality with God's sole causality.

Furthermore, the *mandatum scribendi* is not to be construed in purely 'vertical' terms, as happens when 'writing' is confused with 'dictation', or when inspiration is conceived as a kind of possession or trance, lifting the subject out of the life-connections of history and culture. The *mandatum* is certainly transcendent; it *drives* the writer. Yet it is not mere intrusive and erratic impelling, but the ordering and formation of culture, tradition, occasion and author. Properly understood, 'verbal' inspiration does not extract words from their field of production or reception, does not make the text a less than historical entity, or make the text itself a divine agent. Nor does it entail neglect of the revelatory presence of God in favour of an account of originary inspiration. It simply indicates the inclusion of texts in the sanctifying work of the Spirit so that they may become fitting vessels of the treasure of the gospel.

Conclusion

The force of this chapter has been to suggest that the proper location for a Christian theological account of the nature of Holy Scripture is the Christian doctrine of God. In particular, theological assertions about Scripture are a function of Christian convictions about God's making himself present as saviour and his establishing of covenant fellowship.[48] As Preus puts it in his study of the bibliology of the

---

[48] The importance of God's covenant-forming activity as the context for a doctrine of Scripture has been recently emphasised in M. S. Horton, *Covenant and Eschatology. The Divine Drama* (Louisville: WJKP, 2002), pp. 121–219, and in K. Vanhoozer, *First Theology. God, Scripture and Hermeneutics* (Leicester: Apollos, 2002), pp. 127–203.

orthodox Lutheran divines, the doctrine of Scripture 'assumes its true significance only when viewed soteriologically, when considered as an operative factor in God's plan of salvation'.[49] This saving self-manifestation of God includes within its scope those acts whereby the Spirit of Christ sanctifies and inspires creaturely realities as servants of God's presence. Such Christological-pneumatological clarification of the nature of Scripture enables theology to make the all-important move, that of giving an account of the being of the biblical texts which distinguishes but does not separate them from revelation.[50]

Is all this anything more than a bad case of onto-theology, with logocentric complications? Is it simply one more claim to have the Word of God 'without *courrier*'?[51] The purpose of meticulous dogmatic specification of concepts such as revelation, sanctification and inspiration is precisely to demonstrate that such a charge may only be levelled against coarsely reductive talk of the nature of Holy Scripture. And besides, the Spirit's sanctifying and inspiring work can never be just one more possessed object, one more bit of the Christian cultural climate. Scripture, sanctified and inspired, is the vessel which bears God's majestic presence and is broken in so doing. 'Let not God speak to us, lest we die', say the people of Israel assembled at Sinai (Exod. 20.19); and whatever is said of Scripture must not contravene the eschatological transcendence of the self-revealing God. Of course, a trinitarian account of the matter will not set God's transcendence against his election of creaturely servants, including textual servants. The freedom of God does not annul 'the promise of being able to serve the Word as the Spirit declares it to us'.[52] Yet

---

[49] R. Preus, *The Inspiration of Scripture. A Study of the Theology of the Seventeenth Century Lutheran Dogmaticians* (Edinburgh: Oliver and Boyd, 1957), p. 170.

[50] Cf. Bavinck, *Our Reasonable Faith*, p. 95.

[51] J. Derrida, *The Post Card: From Socrates to Freud and Beyond* (Chicago: University of Chicago Press, 1987), p. 23. Much use is made of Derrida in J. K. A. Smith's somewhat undifferentiated critique of some aspects of the theology of Scripture in *The Fall of Interpretation. Philosophical Foundations for a Creational Hermeneutic* (Downers Grove: InterVarsity Press, 2000).

[52] de Senarclens, *Heirs of the Reformation*, p. 295.

the tension between 'Spirit' and 'letter' may never be completely dissolved, for, like kingship, temple and cult, text also can be lifted out of the history of salvation, isolated from the divine presence, and positivised into a means of handling God. Sanctification and inspiration are not, however, ways of reducing the terror of God's speech, but ways of indicating that what we encounter in Scripture is the terrifying mercy of God's address.

2 | Scripture, Church and Canon

Holy Scripture is an element in the drama of God's redeeming and communicative self-giving. Chapter 1 explored the place of Scripture in that drama by offering dogmatic construals of three aspects of God's activity as lordly and self-presenting saviour: revelation, sanctification and inspiration. Those terms are not to be thought of as referring to essentially separate acts, but to constituent parts of the single yet complex activity through which the triune God vouchsafes his presence, overwhelming sinful ignorance and setting up the light of the knowledge of himself. This second chapter shifts the focus to another dogmatic locus out of which aspects of the nature and office of Holy Scripture are to be determined, namely the doctrine of the church as the creature of the divine Word. The chapter first offers a sketch of some of the primary dogmatic issues – the church as 'hearing church', as 'spiritually visible' and as 'apostolic' – and then gives a more detailed specification of the church of the Word through looking at the authority of Scripture in the church and then at the nature of the church's act of canonisation.

At the beginning of the discussion, however, it is very important to stress that, in proceeding from the doctrine of God's self-revelation to the doctrine of the church, we do not move away from the Christian doctrine of God. Looking at Scripture in terms of the human social space in which it serves the gospel does not entail leaving behind language about the risen Son and the life-giving Spirit which is so indispensable in a theological account of revelation. No less than in talk of revelation, sanctification and inspiration, talk of the human practices of the church must be rooted in, and constantly kept in secure relation to, operative talk of God. At this point – indeed, especially at this point – theology needs to exercise some quite sharp self-discipline if its talk of Scripture is to be authentically theological, and not simply a religiously gilded mixture of social science, history, cultural theory or hermeneutics. Christian theology has a singular preoccupation: God, and everything else *sub specie divinitatis*. All other Christian doctrines are applications or corollaries of the one doctrine, the doctrine of the Trinity, in which the doctrine of the church, no less than the doctrine of revelation, has its proper home.

It is particularly important to emphasise this in view of recent theological discussions of the nature of Scripture (especially on the part of those who might be termed 'post-critical' theologians) which give a high profile to the theme of the church. In such proposals, definition of the character, purpose and interpretation of Scripture is regarded as inseparable from the place occupied by Scripture in the life and practices of the Christian community. Scripture is thus neither a purely formal authority to be invoked in theological deliberation, nor a collection of clues to help us reconstruct its religious and cultural background, nor a symbolic deposit of experience; it is the book of the church, a community text best understood out of its churchly determinacy.

Yet accounts of Scripture as the church's book may contain dogmatic problems. They may be vitiated by a broadly immanentist ecclesiology, one which accords great significance to the church's social visibility, which gives prominence to anthropological concepts such as 'practice' and 'virtue', but which lacks much by way of the instability of a thoroughly eschatological concept of the church. Indeed, such accounts can sometimes take the form of a highly sophisticated hermeneutical reworking of Ritschlian social moralism, in which the centre of gravity of a theology of Scripture has shifted away from God's activity towards the uses of the church. And, accordingly, the preoccupations examined in the previous chapter, all of which focus on God's action through the text, receive only scant treatment; the real interest lies elsewhere, in church practice. But if an account of

Scripture's relation to the life-practices of the church is to have the right kind of dogmatic cogency, it can only be through sustained attention to the fact that ecclesiology is a function of the Christian doctrine of God, and most particularly of the eschatological reality of God's self-gift, whose announcement Scripture serves. The natural correlate of Scripture is not church but revelation. Scripture is not the word of the church; the church is the church of the Word.

Scripture and church: a dogmatic sketch

(1) The definitive act of the church is faithful hearing of the gospel of salvation announced by the risen Christ in the Spirit's power through the service of Holy Scripture. As the *creatura verbi divini*, the creature of the divine Word, the church is the hearing church.

The proper doctrinal context in which our understanding the church, and therefore of the church's relation to Holy Scripture, is to be determined is the relation of Word and faith. 'Word' is a complex term whose usage varies across different areas in which it is put to work, such as Trinity, incarnation or revelation. Here we are using the term to refer to God's self-communication, the revelatory self-gift of the triune God which directs the creation to its saving end. The church exists in the space which is made by the Word. Accordingly, it is not a self-generated assembly and cannot be adequately described only as a human historical trajectory or form of human culture. The church exists and continues because God is communicatively present; it is brought into being and carried by the Word; it *is* (as the Reformers often put it) *solo verbo*. The 'Word' from which the church has its being is thus the lordly creativity of the one who, as Father, Son and Holy Spirit, *calls* into being the things that are not.

To this *solo verbo* there corresponds *sola fide*. In the 1541 Geneva Catechism, Calvin defines faith thus: 'It is a sure and steadfast knowledge of the love of God toward us, according as He declares in His gospel that He is our Father and Saviour (through the mediation of

Jesus Christ).'[1] In a definition such as that offered by Calvin, the external reference of faith is critically important: faith is oriented to that which is outside us and which is antecedent to any attitude we may entertain towards it. The objective reality to which faith turns is here summed up by Calvin as 'the love of God towards us'. Faith entrusts itself to the gospel as to a divine declaration. And because of this basic orientation, faith is not spontaneous; rather, as Calvin states in the answer to the next question in the catechism, faith 'is a singular gift of the Holy Spirit'.[2] Faith, again, is not an original human activity which, when coordinated with a divine activity, establishes fellowship between the believer and God. Faith is itself generated by the fact that God is preveniently 'our God and Father'. This sovereign work of the Spirit, moreover, is necessary because of human sin. What issues from human spontaneity is not faith but wickedness: 'our hearts', Calvin states in the next answer, 'are too prone either to defiance or to a perverse confidence in ourselves or creaturely things'.[3] And so the Spirit 'enlightens', making us capable of understanding, fortifying us with certainty by imprinting the promises of God's salvation on our hearts. By the Spirit, therefore, the church is created as the community of faith, that is, the congregation of those who have been afforded a steady knowledge of the saving love of God. And this work of the Spirit is inseparable from the Word, for that in which Spirit-generated faith places its confidence is the divine promises, that is, the self-declaration or Word of God in the gospel: hence the inseparability of Word alone and faith alone.

What are the consequences of this inseparability of Word and faith for the place of Holy Scripture in the life of the church? The basic ecclesiological effect of the primacy of Word and faith is to give priority to the action of God in the being of the church: 'As the creature of the divine Word the Church is constituted by divine

---

[1] *Geneva Catechism* Q. 111, in T. F. Torrance, ed., *The School of Faith* (London: James Clarke, 1959), p. 22.
[2] *Geneva Catechism* Q. 112, p. 23.   [3] *Geneva Catechism* Q. 113, p. 23.

action.'[4] The church is, therefore, not constituted through human activities and undertakings, but by a reference to the revelatory divine Word and work by which alone it is evoked and maintained in life, for '[i]n accordance with its very *raison d'être*, the church is primordially defined as the *hearing* church'.[5] In concrete terms, this constitution of the church by the divine address as the *hearing* church or the *faithful* assembly means that the presence of Holy Scripture in the life of the church is not the presence of an immanent ecclesial entity. To understand Holy Scripture as without further qualification a part – even the most important part – of the church's cultural capital, its store of meanings, images, foundational narratives, and so on, is seriously to misconstrue the mode of Scripture's operation. Scripture works by forcing the church into an external, 'ecstatic' orientation in all its undertakings; it builds the church up by breaking the church open, and therefore in large measure by breaking the church down. If the church is constituted by the Word, and by Holy Scripture as the Word's servant, then Scripture is an aspect of the church's stability only in so far as that stability is grounded *extra ecclesiam*. For in that externality, in that reference to that which is other than the church and which addresses itself to the church in judgement and mercy, the church has its being; the church *is* outside itself.[6] Scripture is as much a de-stabilising feature of the life of the church as it is a factor in its cohesion and continuity. Defined by Word and faith, the church is not a self-realising institution with Scripture as an instrument of its steady identity. Through Scripture the church is constantly

---

[4] C. Schwöbel, 'The Creature of the Word. Recovering the Ecclesiology of the Reformers', in C. Gunton and D. W. Hardy, eds., *On Being the Church. Essays on the Christian Community* (Edinburgh: T. & T. Clark, 1989), p. 122.

[5] E. Jüngel, 'The Church as Sacrament?', in *Theological Essays 1* (Edinburgh: T. & T. Clark, 1989), p. 205. See, further, E. Jüngel, 'Der Gottesdienst als Fest der Freiheit. Der theologische Ort des Gottesdienstes nach Friedrich Schleiermacher', *Zeichen der Zeit* 38 (1984), pp. 264–72; 'Der evangelisch verstandene Gottesdienst', in *Wertlose Wahrheit. Theologische Erörterungen III* (Munich: Kaiser, 1990), pp. 283–310.

[6] On this, see E. Jüngel, *Das Evangelium von der Rechtfertigung des Gottlosen als Zentrum des christlichen Glaubens* (Tübingen: Mohr, 1998), pp. 64, 77f., 79, 87f.

exposed to interruption. Being the hearing church is never, therefore, a matter of routine, whether liturgical or doctrinal. It is, rather, the church's readiness 'that its whole life should be assailed, convulsed, revolutionised and reshaped'.[7] Holy Scripture is the location of a struggle for the proper externality of the church, for true hearing of the *viva vox Dei*, for true attention to the sanctified and inspired servant through which God announces the judgement and promise of the gospel, above all, for faith as the end of defiance and false confidence and the beginning of humble listening.

(2) The church's visibility, of which Holy Scripture is part, is spiritual visibility.

As the hearing church, the Christian community is wholly referred to the Word of God by which it is established. The church's being is characterised by externality: it is 'ectopic', because its 'place' is in the being and act of the creative and communicative God of the gospel. There is, therefore, a certain strangeness about the church as a form of human life. To live as part of the church is to live at a certain distance from other modes of human fellowship and action. Because it is the creature of the Word, the church is not simply an outgrowth of natural human sociality or religious common interest and fellow-feeling. Its fellowship is properly to be understood as common origination from and participation in the presence of the divine self-gift. And because of this, the church is not primarily a visible social quantity but the invisible new creation. Even in its visible social and historical extension, the church is the presence in history of the new humanity which can never be just one more order of human society. The church is what it is because of the word of the gospel, and so it is primarily spiritual event, and only secondarily visible natural history and structured form of common life. Negatively, this means that the church is 'invisible', that is, not simply identical with its tangible shape as a human social order. Positively, this means that

---

[7] K. Barth, *Church Dogmatics* I/2 (Edinburgh: T. & T. Clark, 1956), p. 804.

the church has true form and visibility in so far as it receives the grace of God through the life-giving presence of Word and Spirit. Its visibility is therefore spiritual visibility.

Holy Scripture participates in this spiritual visibility of the church, serving the self-presence of God. It is not, therefore, simply one more aspect of the ordered statutory life of the community, part of the immanent Christian cultural code, for as a human word it serves the divine Word. This point can best be appreciated by drawing attention to some problematic features of those theologies which tie the nature and function of Scripture very closely to the regularities of ecclesial existence, in effect making the doctrine of Scripture an aspect of the doctrine of the church rather than of the doctrine of revelation.

Some of the difficulties to be discerned in such accounts stem from conflation of the *theological* concept of the church's visibility with the general concept of social externality or positivity. 'The people of God', writes George Lindbeck (who may be taken to exemplify this approach), 'consists of cultural-linguistic groupings that can be meaningfully identified by ordinary sociological and historical criteria.'[8] But against this it must be argued that the church's visibility is not simply an empirical but a spiritual magnitude, and unless it is grasped as this – as *spiritual* visibility – it is not grasped at all,[9] since it is abstracted from the economy of God in which it has its being: the economy of the risen, self-heralding Christ, the economy of the life-giving, sanctifying Spirit. Moreover, if this empirically oriented understanding of visibility becomes dominant in ecclesiology, there are damaging consequences for the way in which Holy Scripture is understood. The place of Scripture in the church comes to be determined out of a general theory of textuality. Corresponding to what is said of the church as social externality, this theory places great emphasis on 'text' as 'external word', that is, as a durable linguistic

[8] G. Lindbeck, 'The Church', in G. Wainwright, ed., *Keeping the Faith* (London: SPCK, 1989), p. 193.

[9] Lindbeck's qualification, to the effect that the 'chosenness' of such socio-linguistic groupings is 'known only to faith' (ibid.) does not take us far enough.

artefact which organises the Christian religious and cultural system, and so shapes Christian thought, speech and action. The functioning of Scripture thus comes to be envisaged in terms of the functioning of other texts of commanding cultural authority: 'Once they penetrate deeply into the psyche, especially the collective psyche, [texts] cease to be primarily objects of study and rather come to supply the conceptual and imaginative vocabularies, as well as the grammar and syntax, in which we construe and construct reality.'[10] The attractiveness of Lindbeck's account derives, of course, from its superiority to those fundamentally Romantic accounts of Scripture which envisage the biblical text as crystallised experience. Its weakness is the dogmatic mislocation of Scripture in ecclesiality. For Lindbeck, Scripture is an instance of the fact that the world's major faiths 'all have relatively fixed canons of writings that they treat as exemplary or normative instantiations of their semiotic code'.[11] But a mistake may be identified here. It is not simply that (as a number of critics have alleged, some rather fiercely) to emphasise 'code' leads to an excessively determinate, 'closed' understanding of the way in which Scripture operates, or that Scripture is separated out from the history (synchronic and diachronic) in which it is 'performed'.[12] But the 'closure' which this construal of Scripture as 'external word' threatens is not so much horizontal as vertical. That is, by treating Scripture as a semiotic *positum* in the culture of the church as visible social entity, it risks severing the transcendent reference of both church and Scripture. Scripture's 'externality' is its reference to revelation, not its

---

[10] G. Lindbeck, 'The Church's Mission to a Postmodern Culture', in F. Burnham, ed., *Postmodern Theology. Christian Faith in a Pluralist World* (New York: Harper, 1988), pp. 39f. On the notion of *verbum externum*, see also G. Lindbeck, 'Barth and Textuality', *Theology Today* 46 (1986), p. 365; *The Nature of Doctrine* (London: SPCK, 1984), pp. 116–20.

[11] Lindbeck, *The Nature of Doctrine*, p. 116.

[12] For a quite nuanced version of this critique, see R. Williams, 'Postmodern Theology and the Judgment of the World', in F. Burnham, ed., *Postmodern Theology. Christian Faith in a Pluralist World* (San Francisco: Harper, 1988), pp. 92–112; 'The Discipline of Scripture', in *On Christian Theology* (Oxford: Blackwell, 2000), pp. 44–59.

visible textuality; that textuality serves the *viva vox Dei*. Attending to Scripture, therefore, is not a matter of being socialised, but of being caught up in the dissolution of all society – including and especially church culture – through the word of the one who smites the earth with the rod of his mouth (cf. Isa. 11.4).

(3) The church's history, of which Holy Scripture is part, is apostolic history.

Because the church's visibility is spiritual visibility, because it is only as God is, acts and speaks, the history of the church is not simply natural history. It is spiritual or, better, 'apostolic' history. To confess that the church is apostolic is to confess that the history of the church is not wholly similar to the histories of other human assemblies and institutions. It is, of course, not wholly dissimilar: to assert that would be to confuse *spiritual* visibility with spiritualised *in*visibility.[13] The church exists in time, and exists as a human undertaking, as a tradition. But what differentiates the life of the church from all other human passage is that it is that history whose impulse lies in the mandate of the risen Christ who commissions and sends. Existing by virtue of this commissioning and sending, and wholly referred to the one who so commissions and sends, the church is apostolic.

The apostolicity of the church is very closely related to its evocation through the Word; to faith as fundamentally constitutive of its relation to its divine source; and to the real character of its visibility. All these ways of speaking of the life of the church locate the centre of its life in the triune God. Apostolicity, similarly, is predicated of the church on the basis of a divine action rather than on the basis of any human dynamic: talk of apostolicity is primarily talk of the church's Lord rather than of the Lord's servants. Nevertheless, the tendency

---

[13] In this sense, N. Healy properly corrects the covert Nestorianism of much modern ecclesiology by emphasising that ecclesiology is a 'practical-prophetic' discipline: see N. M. Healy, *Church, World and Christian Life. Practical-Prophetic Ecclesiology* (Cambridge: Cambridge University Press, 2000), especially pp. 1–51.

to naturalise apostolicity has always been present in the life of the church, most obviously when apostolicity is tied to ordered ministry in such a way that order comes to constitute rather than testify to the apostolic character of the church. So construed, apostolicity is converted into a given form of social order. Properly understood, however, apostolicity is a matter of *being accosted* by a mandate from outside. It is a Christological-pneumatological concept, and only by derivation is it ecclesiological.[14] Apostolicity is the church's standing beneath the imperious directive: 'Go.'

One of the offices of Holy Scripture in the life of the church is to serve this divine directive by giving voice to its inescapable presence. Holy Scripture is one of the points at which the assembly is laid open to the sheer otherness of the divine Word by which it is constituted as the apostolic assembly. This, in the end, is why a strict demarcation between and ordering of Scripture and tradition is required. The demarcation is not, of course, absolute segregation; in one sense there is no pure sphere of biblical textuality wholly independent of the history of the church's acts of reading and reception. But for all this, it is important to maintain that Scripture is not, as it were, swallowed up in or overwhelmed by that history; in its service of the divine Word, Holy Scripture cannot be made into part of the stock of traditional meanings which the church builds up over the course of time. Accordingly, 'tradition' is best conceived of as a *hearing* of the Word rather than a fresh act of *speaking*. 'Nowhere in history is there a "chemically pure Word of God", only a translation of this Word in the preaching of the Church in time.'[15] Thus Yves Congar. Yet to speak thus risks making the Word something lacking in contour, something so porous to the circumstances of its repetition that the fundamental

---

[14] For a perceptive set of reflections on the importance of a Christological (and not simply ecclesiological) account of apostolicity for a theological understanding of the nature of Scripture, see N. Healy, 'Hermeneutics and the Apostolic Form of the Church: David Demson's Question', *Toronto Journal of Theology* 17 (2001), pp. 17–32.

[15] Y. Congar, *Tradition and Traditions* (London: Burns and Oates, 1966), p. 474.

distinction between the apostolic community and the God who calls the community into being is eroded. The Word of God – precisely because it is *God's* Word, God's personal communicative presence – *must* be pure. And Holy Scripture, sanctified and inspired to perform its office, testifies to that Word in the history of the church, so that the church's history becomes apostolic in fresh acts of faith and hearing.

The foregoing is a cumulative attempt to indicate in outline form the nature of the church in which Scripture ministers to the revelation of God: Holy Scripture serves the spiritually visible, apostolic church as the instrument through which the Spirit breaks and reforms the community. Scripture is not the domestic talk of the Christian faith, or simply its familiar semiotic system. It is the sword of God, issuing from the mouth of the risen one. And that is why there can be no 'coinherence of Bible and Church', no 'mutually constitutive reciprocity' between the scriptural witness and the community of the Word, but only of their asymmetry.[16] *Ecclesia nata est ex Dei Verbo.*

These more general considerations on the relation of Scripture and church can now be fleshed out by examining two specific extensions of the dogmatic principles: the authority of Scripture in the church, and the nature of the church's act of canonisation.

The authority of Scripture in the church

The authority of Scripture is its Spirit-bestowed capacity to quicken the church to truthful speech and righteous action. Confession of Scripture's authority is avowal by the hearing church of that which the Spirit undertakes through Scripture's service of the Word, and its proper context is therefore soteriological. From this primary

---

[16] G. Lindbeck, 'Scripture, Consensus, and Community', in R. J. Neuhaus, ed., *Biblical Interpretation in Crisis* (Grand Rapids: Eerdmans, 1989), p. 78.

definition flow all other aspects of Scripture's authority, such as its role in theological or moral argument, its place in proclamation, or its liturgical presence.

Truthful speech and righteous action are a following of the order of reality, ways of engaging with the world which follow its inherent nature and the ends which it displays to us. That which has authority is that which legitimately directs us to those ends, and so that which both forms and judges action. Authority is political because it shapes social relations; but true political authority is neither capricious nor arbitrary but lawful and *fitting to reality*. Authority is potent because it bears the truth to and therefore orders our acts, whether intellectual or practical, in accordance with reality. And so authority cannot be conferred; authorisation is not a proposal, but an act of truthful judgement through which authority is acknowledged as that which rightly kindles activity of a specific quality in a specific direction.

That authority is properly a matter for *acknowledgement* is especially important in discussing the nature of Scripture's authority in the church. Very simply, the church is not competent to confer authority on Holy Scripture, any more than it is competent to be a speaking church before it is a hearing church, or competent to give itself the mandate to be apostolic. The authority of Scripture is not another way of talking about the accumulated *gravitas* which has been acquired by Scripture through the church's use. Acknowledgement of the authority of Scripture is not simply an after-the-event acknowledgement of what the church's custom has come to be in the way it governs its life by a particular set of texts; *de facto* authority is only of any real force if it is grounded in *de jure* authority. If it is not so grounded, then not only does Scripture become simply tradition, but the authority of Scripture lays itself open to critique as an arbitrary exercise of social power.

The modern historicist critique of authority as only a political postulate has been readily applied to the biblical texts. Most notably was it so applied by Kant in contrasting the poor benighted 'biblical theologian' working within the confining wall of 'ecclesiastical faith, which is based on statutes'[17] and the rational theologian who strides through 'the free and open fields of private judgement and philosophy'.[18] The authority of a text, in other words, is for Kant merely 'based on statutes – that is, on laws proceeding from another person's act of choice'.[19] Such a framework finds expression in a characteristic statement from a contemporary treatment of biblical authority: 'Where texts are accepted as authoritative within a community it is the community's authority that is invested in them.'[20] There is an entire modern understanding of authority in that statement: nominalist in its isolation of authority from the way the world is, and constructivist in thinking of biblical authority as 'invested' in the texts by the church. Of course, we would be foolish to be deaf to the protest against the authoritarian abuse of biblical authority voiced by Kant and his contemporary heirs. But the abuse of biblical authority, its use as a weapon for social wickedness, cannot be countered by stripping Scripture of any inherent authority and converting claims about Scripture into claims about the community. To do that is not to solve the problem of abuse but to repeat it, for Scripture still remains a function of society, whether that society be the benighted community of ecclesiastical faith or the free enlightened 'learned public'.[21] What is needed, rather, is a dogmatic move: the reintegration of the authority of Scripture into the doctrine of God, which will have the effect of decisively redrawing the character of the church's affirmation of Scripture's authority, removing that affirmation from the sphere of the politics of invention, and restricting the church's office to the pedagogical one of confessing or attesting that

---

[17] I. Kant, *The Conflict of the Faculties*, in A. W. Wood and G. Di Giovanni, eds., *Religion and Rational Theology* (Cambridge: Cambridge University Press, 1996), p. 262.

[18] Ibid., p. 252.   [19] Ibid., p. 262.

[20] R. Morgan with J. Barton, *Biblical Interpretation* (Oxford: Oxford University Press, 1988), p. 7.

[21] Kant, *The Conflict of the Faculties*, p. 261.

Scripture's authority flows from its given place in the economy of grace.[22]

This is not to suggest that the authority of Scripture can be abstracted from the life and acts of the church as the place where the saving presence of God is encountered. To lift the authority of Scripture out of the context of the church would be to formalise that authority by abstracting Scripture from its revelatory and therefore ecclesial setting.[23] Such formalisation often happens if the notion of inspiration is allowed to expand beyond its proper limits in such a way that the authority of Scripture becomes a function of the manner of its (inspired) production rather than of Scripture's service to the authoritative divine Word of revelation. Authority, that is, becomes something derived from a formal property of Scripture – its perfection as divine product – rather than of its employment in the divine service. And the perception of authority does indeed become akin to mute obedience to statute. In the end, this reduces authority to a 'formal supernaturalism'[24] insufficiently integrated into Scripture's role as the bearer of the gospel of salvation to the church. An effective account of biblical authority, by contrast, will place it within a cluster of other affirmations: God as sanctifying, inspiring and authorising presence; the Spirit as the one who enables recognition of, trust in and glad submission to the claim of Scripture's gospel content; the

---

[22] It is along these dogmatic lines that one would need to develop a response to the critique of the concept and function of biblical authority mounted by, e.g., E. Farley, *Ecclesial Reflection. An Anatomy of Theological Method* (Philadelphia: Fortress Press, 1982), pp. 47–82, or F. Wagner, 'Auch der Teufel zitiert die Bibel. Das Christentum zwischen Autoritätsanspruch und Krise des Schriftprinzips', in R. Ziegert, ed., *Die Zukunft des Schriftprinzips* (Stuttgart: Deutsche Bibelgesellschaft, 1994), pp. 236–58. Both accounts suffer from dogmatic abstraction in construing biblical authority, and both force the historical material into too schematic a narrative. By contrast, A. Wenz ties Scripture's authority to personal divine presence in *Das Wort Gottes* (see, e.g., p. 301).

[23] For an account of this process, see the important essay by T. F. Torrance, 'The Deposit of Faith', *Scottish Journal of Theology* 36 (1983), pp. 1–28.

[24] E. Schlink, *Theology of the Lutheran Confessions* (Philadelphia: Fortress Press, 1961), p. 10, n. 4.

church as faithful, self-renouncing and confessing assembly around the lively Word of God.

In a closely connected way, the formalisation of Scripture's authority can take place when the juridical function of Scripture in theological polemic is abstracted from its soteriological function, that is, from the content of Scripture as the gospel of salvation and the directedness of Scripture towards the enabling of life in truthful fellowship with God through the ordering of the church's speech and action. Talk of the authority of Scripture is practical and teleological, inseparable from the church's existence in faithful submission to the gospel's declaration that God is (as Calvin put it in the catechism) 'our Father and Saviour (through the mediation of Jesus Christ)'.

There is an important consequence here for the manner in which the authority of Scripture is apprehended by the church. The church's submission to the gospel is not accomplished simply by notional affirmations of Scripture's formal-juridical status in the church. Indeed, such notional affirmations can be the enemy of true spiritual confession, tempting the church to think that confession is a finished business rather than 'a continuous evangelical mandate'.[25] Confession of Scripture's authority is part of the church's existence in grateful and repentant acknowledgement of the *benevolentia Dei* through the Spirit's gift. It is not that dull-witted conformity to external ordinance of which Kant was (rightly) contemptuous; nor is it subjection to the letter. It is glad affirmation of the force of *sola gratia* and *sola fide* in the realm of the knowledge of the gospel.

To sum up: the authority of Scripture is the authority of the church's Lord and his gospel, and so cannot be made an immanent feature of ecclesial existence. Scripture's authority *within* the church is a function of Scripture's authority *over* the church.[26] The

---

[25] G. C. Berkouwer, *Holy Scripture* (Grand Rapids: Eerdmans, 1975), p. 36.

[26] This is why it is proper to talk of Scripture's authority as *in se* (see R. Preus, *The Inspiration of Scripture. A Study of the Theology of the Seventeenth Century Lutheran*

church's acknowledgement of Scripture's authority is not an act of self-government, but an exposure to judgement, to a source not simply of authorisation but also and supremely of interrogation. A church in which it makes sense to say: *scriptura sacra locuta, res decisa est* is the antithesis of a stable, statutory human project; it is, rather, a form of common life centred on a confession which subverts. Hence a church of the Word cannot be a closed, static set of relations, a social space characterised by maximal local cohesion and historical durability. It is an 'open' culture. But its openness is not secured by stressing its indeterminacy, or its character as unfinished and unfinishable project, as in some postmodern cultural theory. The church's openness is its subjection to prophecy, its being opened *ab extra* by the interceptive Word of God. What prevents church life from drifting into idolatrous closure is the fact that its 'space' is the economy of God's self-presence, in which it is subject to the interruption of scriptural testimony. 'Revelation is not a development of our religious ideas but their continuous conversion', said H. Richard Niebuhr;[27] and 'life in the presence of revelation . . . is not lived before or after but in the midst of a great revolution'.[28] It is the office of Holy Scripture to bring that revolution to bear upon the church, and the office of the church to acknowledge this fearsome gift of grace. '*Ecclesia non est magistra, sed ministra scripturae; non mater, sed filia; non autor, sed custos, testis et interpres; non judex, sed index et vindex.*'[29]

Dogmaticians (Edinburgh: Oliver and Boyd, 1957), pp. 88f.) as a protection against subsuming Scripture under the church; the notion of Scripture's *in se* authority only becomes problematical when it is extracted from, on the one hand, considerations of divine action *through* Scripture, and, on the other hand, the directedness of Scripture to the building up of the saving fellowship of God and humankind.

[27] H. R. Niebuhr, *The Meaning of Revelation* (New York: Macmillan, 1962), p. 182.

[28] Ibid., p. 183.

[29] D. Hollaz, *Examen theologicum acroamaticum* (1741), cited by Preus, *The Inspiration of Scripture*, p. 98, n. 3.

Canonisation

In the light of the fact that, as hearer of the Word, the church is 'not judge but testifier and vindicator of Scripture', how is the church's act of canonisation to be dogmatically described? The central issue in this matter (forced upon theology with fresh force by historical accounts of the canon) is, as Berkouwer puts it, 'the relationship between the canon as both norm and authority and the human considerations that can be discerned in the history of the canon'.[30] There can be no recourse to denials of the element of human decision-making in the process of canonisation.[31] To make such a move would not only idealise or spiritualise the canon in the way that older theories of inspiration often threatened to do, but also deny that it really is human texts and human textual activity which are sanctified by God. That human activity includes those processes to which we refer in shorthand terms as 'canonisation'.[32] What is needed, by contrast, is a theological account of the church's action at this point; we need to give a dogmatic answer to the question of 'the nature of the human activity which can be denoted as the "accepting", the *recipere* of the canon'.[33] Such an answer will provide both a general dogmatic picture of the landscape within which that decision takes place and a more precise, focussed depiction of the act itself.

In portraying the larger field which encompasses this decision of the church, it is very important not to begin with the church or with

---

[30] Berkouwer, *Holy Scripture*, p. 70.

[31] One of the weaknesses of E. Herms' controversial essay 'Was haben wir an der Bibel? Versuch einer Theologie des christlichen Kanons', *Jahrbuch für biblische Theologie* 12 (1998), pp. 99–152, is its underlying dualist assumption that a functionalist or socio-pragmatic account of the canon can only proceed by the exclusion of theological considerations. For a pointed critique of Herms, see M. Welker, 'Sozio-metaphysische Theologie und Biblische Theologie. Zu Eilert Herms: "Was haben wir an der Bibel?"', *Jahrbuch für biblische Theologie* 13 (1999), pp. 309–22.

[32] It is, of course, important, not to be beguiled into thinking of canonisation as a single event or decision: it is more akin to a muddled set of interwoven processes.

[33] Berkouwer, *Holy Scripture*, p. 72.

the texts of the Bible. Dogmatic order involves depicting the church's
act out of Christology and pneumatology.

Canonisation, first, is to be understood in terms of the church's
character as assembly around the self-bestowing presence of the risen
Christ. In particular, this act of the church is enclosed within the
prophetic presence and activity of Jesus Christ. The primary speech-
act which takes place within the church and from which all other
churchly speech-acts derive is Jesus Christ's own self-utterance. That
self-utterance is mediated through the language of prophetic testimony to which Scripture bears witness and which then forms the
basis and norm of the church's public speech. But it is all-important
to emphasise that this mediation does not mean that Jesus Christ
is replaced as speaker by some human text or official, or that he is
mute until the church speaks – any more than the mediation of the
beneficia Christi through sacraments means that Jesus Christ's saving
work is inert until sacramentally realised, or that it is the church's
sacramental action which renders Christ present and effective. '[I]n
the apostles as the receiving end of His revealing and reconciling
activity, Jesus Christ laid the foundation of the Church which He in-
corporated into Himself as His own Body, and permitted the Word
which He put into their mouth to take the form of proclamation
answering to and extending His own in such a way that it became
the controlled unfolding of His own revelation within the mind and
language of the apostolic foundation.'[34]

An account of the canon and canonisation is therefore an account
of the extension of Christ's active, communicative presence in the
Spirit's power through the commissioned apostolic testimony. And,
moreover, an account of the church's canonising acts has to be rooted
in the facts that (as we have said) the church is properly a hearing
church before it is a speaking church, and that even its speech, when
it is properly apostolic, is always contingent upon and indicative of

[34] T. F. Torrance, 'The Word of God and the Response of Man', in *God and Rationality*
(Oxford: Oxford University Press, 1971), p. 152.

a prior speech-act. Its speech is generated and controlled by Christ's self-utterance. '[T]here exists prior to and above and after every *ego dico* and *ecclesia dicit* a *haec dixit Dominus*; and the aim of Church proclamation is that this *haec dixit Dominus* should prevail and triumph, not only before, above and after, but also *in* every *ego dico* and *ecclesia dicit*.'[35]

Second, therefore, if the church's speech is governed by the self-communication of Christ, the church's acts of judgement (its 'decisions') are governed by the Holy Spirit who animates the church and enables its perception of the truth. The role of pneumatology is primarily to 'de-centre' the church's act of canonisation, in two ways. Talk of the Spirit is a means of identifying the providential activity of God in the history of the Christian community, including the history of its relation to and treatment of the biblical texts. 'We should', wrote Schleiermacher, 'conceive of the Spirit as ruling and guiding in the thought-world of the whole Christian body just as each individual does in his own . . . [T]he faithful preservation of the apostolic writings is the work of the Spirit of God acknowledging his own products.'[36] And talk of the Spirit is also a means of identifying that the perception of canonicity derives not simply from the natural *sensus communis* of the church but from the charismatic gift of 'the sense for the truly apostolic'.[37] In this light, what description is to be offered of the 'great and meritorious act' of canonisation?

We begin from Calvin:

> I wittingly pass over what they teach on the power to approve Scripture. For to subject the oracles of God in this way to men's judgment,

---

[35] Barth, *Church Dogmatics* I/2 p. 801. Cf. O. Weber, *Foundations of Dogmatics*, vol. I (Grand Rapids: Eerdmans, 1981), p. 249.

[36] F. Schleiermacher, *The Christian Faith* (Edinburgh: T. & T. Clark, 1928), p. 602; cf. I. Dorner, *A System of Christian Doctrine*, vol. IV (Edinburgh: T. & T. Clark, 1882), p. 247.

[37] Schleiermacher, *The Christian Faith*, p. 603.

making their validity depend upon human whim, is a blasphemy unfit to be mentioned.[38]

[A] most pernicious error widely prevails that scripture has only so much weight as is conceded to it by the consent of the church. As if the eternal and inviolable truth of God depended upon the decision of men![39]

That it is the proper office of the Church to distinguish genuine from spurious Scripture, I deny not, and for this reason, that the Church obediently embraces whatever is of God. The sheep hear the voice of the shepherd, and will not listen to the voice of strangers. But to submit the sound oracles of God to the Church, that they may obtain a kind of precarious authority among men, is blasphemous impiety. The Church is, as Paul declares, founded on the doctrine of Apostles and Prophets; but these men speak as if they imagined that the mother owed her birth to the daughter.[40]

Calvin's well-known objection to one interpretation of Augustine's dictum that 'I should not believe the gospel except as moved by the authority of the catholic church'[41] is partly, of course, an objection to a certain construal of the authority of the church. But there is something deeper here: what Calvin fears is that to assert that Scripture takes its approbation from the church is radically to misinterpret the character of the church's act with respect to the canon. It is not that he denies that the church does, indeed, 'approve' Scripture, but more that such an act of approval is, properly understood, a receptive

[38] J. Calvin, *Institutes of the Christian Religion* iv.9.xiv (Philadelphia: Westminster Press, 1960), p. 1178.

[39] Ibid., 1.7.i (p. 75).

[40] J. Calvin, 'The True Method of Giving Peace to Christendom and of Reforming the Church', in *Tracts and Treatises in Defence of the Reformed Faith*, vol. iii (Edinburgh: Oliver and Boyd, 1958), p. 267.

[41] Augustine, *Against the Epistle of Manichaeus called Fundamental* 5, in *Writings Against the Manichaeans and Against the Donatists* (Edinburgh: T. & T. Clark, 1989), p. 31.

rather than an authorising act. Hence two features of the church's act of approval are of critical importance for Calvin. First, it is derived from the Spirit's presence in the church, and therefore by no means autonomous. 'They mock the Holy Spirit', Calvin says, 'when they ask . . . Who can persuade us to receive one book in reverence but to exclude another, unless the church prescribe a sure rule for all these matters?'[42]: hence his development of the doctrine of the *testimonium internum Spiritus Sancti* as a pneumatological replacement for the idea of ecclesial approbation. But, second, the church's act with respect to the canon is an act of faithful *assent* rather than a self-derived judgement. The language of discipleship is not incidental here: affirming the canon is a matter of the church 'obediently embracing' what comes from God, or of the sheep hearing the shepherd's voice; that is, it is an act of humble affirmation of and orientation towards what is already indisputably the case in the sphere of salvation and its communication in human speech. '[W]hile the church receives and gives its seal of approval to the Scriptures, it does not thereby render authentic what is otherwise doubtful or controversial. But because the church recognizes Scripture to be the truth of its own God, as a pious duty it unhesitatingly venerates Scripture.'[43] Once again: none of this is a denial that canonisation is the church's act; it is simply an attempt to specify what *kind* of act. The problem with naturalistic accounts of canonisation is not that they show that establishing the canon is a matter of policy, but that – like Calvin's opponents – policy becomes arbitrary *poiesis*: whim, judgement, decision, rather than normed compliance. How may this act of compliant judgement be more closely described? Four characteristics can be identified.

First, the church's judgement is an act of confession of that which precedes and imposes itself on the church (that is, the *viva vox Jesu Christi* mediated through the apostolic testimony) and which evokes

[42] Calvin, *Institutes of the Christian Religion* I.vii.1 (p. 75).   [43] Ibid., I.vii.2 (p. 76).

a Spirit-guided assent. The church's 'decision' with respect to the canon is thus 'simultaneously its acknowledgement of something which it is receiving from an authority over it'.[44] Only in a secondary sense is canonisation an act of selection, authorisation or commendation on the church's part, for 'it is not for us or for any man to constitute this or that writing as Holy Writ, as the witness to God's revelation, to choose it as such out of many others, but . . . if there is such a witness and the acceptance of such a witness, it can only mean that it has already been constituted and chosen, and that its acceptance is only the discovery and acknowledgment of this fact'.[45] The 'decision' of the church is not a matter of pure *arbitrium*, but of *arbitrium liberatum*. To put it differently: this decision has noetic but not ontological force, acknowledging what Scripture is but not making it so.[46]

Second, this act of confession, the church's judgement with respect to the canon, is an act of submission before it is an act of authority. This is because the authority of the church is nothing other than its acknowledgement of the norm under which it stands. 'The Church has exactly as much authority as it exercises obedience.'[47] Robert Jenson's recent and rather startling account of the canon falls at just this point: it fails to give sufficient theological specificity to the notion of 'decision'. 'The canon of Scripture . . . is . . . a dogmatic decision of the church. If we will allow no final authority to churchly dogma, or to the organs by which the church can enunciate dogma, there can be no canon of Scripture. The slogan *sola scriptura*, *if* by that is meant "apart from creed, teaching office, or authoritative liturgy" is an oxymoron.'[48] But does not this subvert

---

[44] Weber, *Foundations of Dogmatics*, vol. 1, p. 251.

[45] Barth, *Church Dogmatics* 1/2, p. 473. See also E. Schlink, *Ökumenische Dogmatik. Grundzüge* (Göttingen: Vandenhoeck und Ruprecht, 1983), p. 634.

[46] For this distinction, see Berkouwer, *Holy Scripture*, p. 78.

[47] Weber, *Foundations of Dogmatics*, vol. 1, p. 251.

[48] R. Jenson, *Systematic Theology*, vol. 1 (Oxford: Oxford University Press, 1997), pp. 27f.

the very affirmation it seeks to make, by construing the church's act of judgement as 'a historically achieved commendation by the church as community to the church as association of persons',[49] and not as an act of deference to that which moves the judgement of the church from without? And how may the church resist its persistent desire to be in monologue with itself unless its 'authoritative' decision with respect to the canon is its avowal of a norm beneath which it already stands and beneath which it can only stand if it is to perceive the truth?

Third, as an act of confession and submission, the act of canonisation has a *backward* reference. Through it, the church affirms that all truthful speech in the church can proceed only from the prior apostolic testimony. Canonisation is recognition of apostolicity, not simply in the sense of the recognition that certain texts are of apostolic authorship or provenance, but, more deeply, in the sense of the confession that these texts, 'grounded in the salvific act of God in Christ which has taken place once for all',[50] are annexed to the self-utterance of Jesus Christ. The canon and the apostolicity (and so the apostolic succession) of the church are inseparable here. 'The apostolic succession of the Church must mean that it is guided by the Canon.'[51] The wider ecclesiological point – so easily obscured in ecclesiologies which take their cues from socio-historical depictions of the immanent dynamics of communities – is that the church and all its acts are *ostensive*, pointing beyond and behind themselves to that which transcends and precedes them. Thus '[t]he canonic decision of the Church is essentially its confession of the norm already given it, the standard by which it was prepared to let itself be measured . . . The canon is an expression of the fact that the Church is only in reference backward actually the Church.'[52]

Fourth, as an act of confession, submission and retrospection, the church's judgement with respect to the canon is its pledging of itself to

[49] Ibid., p. 28.   [50] Schlink, *Ökumenische Dogmatik*, p. 635.
[51] Barth, *Church Dogmatics* I/1, p. 104.
[52] Weber, *Foundations of Dogmatics*, vol. I, p. 252.

be carried by this norm in all its actions. Canonisation is commitment to operate by a given norm, and thereby to have speech and action mastered by that norm. In a very real sense, the canon spells the end of free speech in the church, if by free speech we mean mere *Willkür*; the canon means obligation to appeal to the canon and be ruled by it in such a way that the freedom of the norm is not transgressed but kept in view at every moment as the norm is applied and operated. One consequence here is that the church's *use* of the canon has a distinctively passive character (not usually stated with any clarity in much talk of the 'uses of Scripture'). In an influential essay, Kendall Folkert drew a distinction between a canon of texts which is carried by other religious activity, 'present in a tradition principally by the force of a vector or vectors', and a canon of texts which is the carrier of other religious activities, that is, 'normative texts that are more independently and distinctively present within a tradition . . . and which themselves often function as vectors'.[53] A Christian account of the canon is of the latter variety, because canonicity is not a function of use but use a function of canonicity (which is itself a function of divine approbation and use). Affirmation of the canon is thus a commitment to allow all the activities of the church (most of all, its acts of worship, proclamation and ruling) to be as it were enclosed by the canon. Worship, proclamation and ruling do not *make use* of the canon, as if it were a catalogue of resources through which the church could browse and from which it could select what it considered fitting or tasteful for some particular occasion; rather, they are acts which are at all points shaped by the canon and what it sets before the church.

Taken together, these four considerations suggest that, theologically construed – construed, that is, with an eye to its place in the history of the saving self-communication of the triune God – the church's act of canonisation is a set of human activities, attitudes and

---

[53] K. W. Folkert, 'The "Canons" of "Scripture"', in M. Levering, ed., *Rethinking Scripture* (Albany: SUNY Press, 1989), p. 173.

relations which refer beyond themselves to prevenient divine acts of speaking and sanctifying. Like any other element in the church – oversight, service, proclamation, prayer, sacraments, fellowship, witness – the canon is a matter of grace, of a divine promise attached to a creaturely reality. And like all those elements, the canon, too, is 'a playground of human self-will'; but it is also 'the sphere of the lordship of Christ', and so

> If we believe that the Lord is mightier than the sin which indisputably reigns in the Church, if we believe that He is the victor in the struggle against grace which is indisputably widespread even in the Church, then we can count on it that a genuine knowledge and confession in respect of the Canon, and therefore a knowledge and confession of the genuine Canon, is not at least impossible in the Church, not because we have to believe in men, but because if we are not to give up our faith we have to believe in the miracle of grace.[54]

In sum: our appeal here has been to a number of related ecclesiological concepts – the church as faithful hearer of the divine Word, as spiritually visible, as apostolic – which form the framework of an account of the authority of the scriptural canon in the church. The Word–faith–church nexus, for all its deep roots in classical Protestant dogmatics, has become less than familiar, its place often occupied by sophisticated theories of communal tradition and practice. Such theories are not doctrinally neutral, as we shall see when in the next chapter we turn to examine their application to hermeneutics, and it is precisely the doctrinal tug that they exert which makes the development of a distinctly dogmatic account a matter of some necessity. 'Without Scripture there is no church, for as communion with Christ the church lives from the common faith of its members in Jesus Christ. But without God's Word there is no faith, without faith there is no church, and without

[54] Barth, *Church Dogmatics* 1/2, p. 598.

Scripture no knowledge of the Word of God which creates faith.'[55] What does this mean for the way in which Holy Scripture is to be read?

[55] I. U. Dalferth, 'Die Mitte ist außen. Anmerkungen zum Wirklichkeitsbezug evangelischer Schriftauslegung', in C. Landmesser et al., eds., *Jesus Christus als die Mitte der Schrift. Studien zur Hermeneutik des Evangeliums* (Berlin: de Gruyter, 1977), p. 175.

3 | Reading in the Economy of Grace

There is a certain intellectual dignity and stateliness to the theological
concepts which we have been exploring so far. But their appeal is also
spiritual. Revelation, sanctification, inspiration, canon cannot be fittingly handled as just so much dogmatic apparatus; understanding
them is inseparable from their Christian deployment. We may, therefore, begin with a statement from one of the old Lutheran divines on
the 'use' of the article on Scripture:

> This article is to be used in the following manner: We are to recognize
> and accept without reservation the holy Scripture . . . as the Word
> of Almighty God, and we are to regard and cherish it as the most
> precious of treasures . . . We are devoutly to give audience to God
> speaking in the Word, we are to reflect upon His Word day and night
> and we are to explore it with true piety and utmost devotion . . . We
> are to turn neither to the right nor to the left from Scripture, nor
> are we to suffer ourselves to be moved to the slightest degree by the
> solicitation of others or the desires of our own flesh, lest in some way
> we introduce something in doctrine or life which is contrary to better
> knowledge or against our conscience . . . We are to gain comfort from
> them alone in every necessity of body and soul, and through patient
> consolation of the Scriptures have a sure hope of life and remain
> steadfast to the end of life.[1]

---

[1] A. Calov, *Systema* 1, 517, cit. from R. Preus, *The Inspiration of Scripture. A Study of the
Theology of the Seventeenth Century Lutheran Dogmaticians* (Edinburgh: Oliver and
Boyd, 1957), p. 12.

There are few clearer or more moving descriptions of the fact that for a classical Protestant dogmatician like Calov, Christian teaching about the nature of Holy Scripture was no mere formal principle of knowledge but rather a piece of practical, spiritual counsel. Rightly grasping the nature of Scripture involves both rational assent and a pious disposition of mind, will and affections. Recognition, acceptance, giving audience, devotion, a checking of distracting desire, faith, trust, a looking to Scripture for consolation: such attitudes and practices are to characterise the faithful reader of Scripture, and their absence denotes a degenerate understanding of what is involved in reading it.

If, however, we ourselves are to talk in this way, we must shake ourselves free from an entire intellectual and spiritual culture, a culture in which the humble, chastened actions and attitudes recommended by Calov have little place. To set out the issues, this chapter draws a contrast between a representative modern account of what might be termed the 'anthropology of reading' – that of Schopenhauer – and two contrary witnesses, one early modern and one relatively recent – Calvin and Bonhoeffer.[2] On the basis of this contrast, we move on to a dogmatic sketch of what it means to be a reader of Scripture in the economy of divine grace. It is important at the beginning to register that, as with the doctrine of the church, so here in discussing the nature of reading: we do not move away from operative language about God, shifting into territory more effectively mapped by a psychology of interpretation, a theory of virtue or, perhaps, a general account of

---

[2] For a more encompassing account of the breakdown of reading texts as Scripture, see W. Kort, *'Take, Read'. Scripture, Textuality, and Cultural Practice* (University Park: Pennsylvania State University Press, 1996), pp. 37–67. Kort argues that reading the Bible as Scripture declines as classical practices of reading are extended from Scripture first to the book of nature, then to history and finally to literature, in ways which subvert the primacy of the Bible and which eventually come to set the terms within which the Bible is read. Kort does not draw attention, however, to the doctrinal shifts which accompany this process (most of all, the extraction of accounts of the nature of the Bible from the revelatory activity of God).

rational acts. Language about the merciful self-presence of the triune God has as much work to do when we are talking about readers as it does when we are talking about revelation and its textual servants. And therefore here, too, dogmatics is doubly important. First, dogmatics will prove itself a capable assistant in the genealogical task, that is, in the task of unearthing and exposing to critical inspection conventions whose very self-evidence obscures them from view. Precisely because of its jaggedness – the fact that it cannot readily be fitted into or coordinated with some pervasive cultural assumptions – dogmatics has the potential to alert us to the contingency of those assumptions and to suggest an account of their provenance. Second, dogmatics offers a means of producing a portrait of the economy of grace, and of humankind and its activities in that economy, free from anxieties about foundations and therefore at liberty to devote itself to the descriptive task with Christian alertness, clarity and joy.[3]

The task before us, then, is to portray what Calov calls right 'use' of Holy Scripture as the sanctified servant of God in which the gospel is set before the attentive church. If Scripture is the servant of the Word and the church is the hearer of the Word, what is involved in reading this text? How may we specify the reader's activity in dogmatic terms? There can, of course, be no doubt that there *is* such an activity. Scripture does not exist in abstraction from its readers. This is because Scripture is an auxiliary in the economy of salvation, and the end of that economy is *fellowship*. Salvation is reconciliation, and as such includes the healing and restoration of communicative fellowship between God and humankind, broken by the creature's defiance and ignorance. But communicative fellowship cannot be healed on one

[3] Although there is an abundance of material on the nature of reading in the fields of literary and cultural studies, the literature in religious studies is comparatively modest, and in theology decidedly thin. Theological accounts include K. Huizing, *Homo legens. Vom Ursprung der Theologie im Lesen* (Berlin: de Gruyter, 1996), and A. T. Khoury and L. Muth, eds., *Glauben durch Lesen? Für eine christliche Lesekultur* (Freiburg: Herder, 1990). See also the important study by P. Griffiths, *Religious Reading. The Place of Reading in the Practice of Religion* (Oxford: Oxford University Press, 1999), and Kort, 'Take, Read'.

side only; it must include the restoration of the human partner to a genuine participation in the knowledge of God. Grace, of course, is always unidirectional, and our restoration by grace to the knowledge of God comes from God alone, in the work of the redeeming Son and the quickening Spirit. But what grace creates *ex nihilo* by raising humankind from the dead is not a mere empty space, an *absence*, for then there would be no creaturely counterpart to the self-gift of God. Grace establishes fellowship; and consequently the economy of revelatory grace includes the sanctification of the human knower, so that through the Spirit his or her knowing is ordered towards God. This, as we have seen, is why an account of God's revelatory self-presence must necessarily be completed by an account of the church which is the first fruit of God's utterance, and why the 'hearing' church is not simply a passive reality but also – under the rule of God – a community which engages in visible acts. And furthermore, this is why an account of readers and reading in the economy of grace is a necessary ingredient in a theological account of the place of Holy Scripture in the economy of salvation, for the act of reading Scripture is an aspect of the covenant mutuality to which human-kind is restored and in which creaturely acts find their proper place.

Because of this, a good deal of attention needs to be given to offering a depiction of those creaturely acts – including acts of read-ing – with the right kind of Christian particularity.[4] In defining the church's acts of authorisation and canonisation, two things proved especially important: first, not to assume that non-dogmatic ac-counts of social process could be imported into a theological de-scription without heavy revision, and second, to allow the real work to be done by doctrines. Similarly, in defining what it means to *read* Scripture in the economy of grace, we shall not be able to make much headway if we determine in advance of any dogmatic considerations what 'reading' is, and then seek to apply such a determination to the

---

[4] On the need to resist the assimilation of all reading-acts to one standard model, see Griffiths, *Religious Reading*.

church's encounter with Scripture. The act of reading Scripture – because it is the act of reading *Scripture*, the herald of the *viva vox Dei* – is not an instance of something else, but an act which, though it is analogous to other acts, is in its deepest reaches *sui generis*. For as with all Christian acts, its substance is in the last analysis determined not out of its similarities to the acts of other agents who do not share the Christian confession, but by the formative economy of salvation in which it has its origin and end. In that formative economy, the act of reading partakes of the basic structure of Christian existence, namely its active passivity or passive activity. Like other acts of Christian existence it is a human activity whose substance lies in its reference to and self-renunciation before the presence and action of God.

The act of reading Holy Scripture thus contains a certain self-negation. The *epoche* involved in Christian reading of Scripture is, of course, something which in some respects it shares with other acts of reading, and something which explains the uneasy place which reading has in some strands of the culture of modernity. Reading does not cohere well with the ideal of spontaneous and self-possessive individuality which is one of the hallmarks of modern anthropology. To illustrate the point we may consider some remarks from Schopenhauer:

> The difference between the effect produced on the mind by thinking for yourself and that produced by reading is incredibly great . . . For reading forcibly imposes on the mind thoughts that are as foreign to its mood as the signet is to the wax upon which it impresses its seal. The mind is totally subjected to an external compulsion to think this or that for which it has no inclination and is not in the mood . . . The result is that *much* reading robs the mind of all elasticity, as the continual pressure of a weight does a spring, and that the surest way of never having any thoughts of your own is to pick up a book every time you have a free moment.[5]

[5] A. Schopenhauer, *Essays and Aphorisms* (Harmondsworth: Penguin, 1970), pp. 89f.

What is so instructive in the contrast which Schopenhauer draws between 'thinking for yourself' and 'reading' is the underlying ideal of intellectual originality, in the deep sense that intellectual activity is only authentic when it is uncoerced. Real thinking is 'for yourself', that is, an act of the will. Like a spring, the mind has its own stored energy, and retains that power only in so far as it is not weighed down. Reading erodes spontaneity, subjecting the thinker to an 'external compulsion' and the forcible imposition of what is 'alien'. Thinking, by contrast, is proper to us. 'Fundamentally it is only our own basic thoughts that possess truth and life, for only these do we really understand through and through. The thoughts of another that we have read are crumbs from another's table, the cast-off clothes of an unfamiliar guest.'[6] And so '[r]eading is merely a surrogate for thinking for yourself: it means letting someone else direct your thoughts . . . To banish your own thoughts so as to take up a book is a sin against the Holy Ghost.'[7] Behind such statements lie two profound anthropological ideas: immediacy and autonomy. 'The characteristic mark of minds of the first rank', Schopenhauer notes, 'is the immediacy of all their judgements.'[8] Judgement is thus not learned but self-derived – things learned are for Schopenhauer like 'an artificial limb, a false tooth, a wax nose'.[9] The thinker is lord of himself; and so 'He who truly thinks for himself . . . no more accepts authorities than a monarch does orders . . . His judgements, like the decisions of a monarch, arise directly from his own absolute power.'[10] This, in the end, is why for Schopenhauer – as for Descartes[11] – genuine thinkers are *thinkers for themselves*.[12] But a Christian theological account of reading Scripture must beg to differ, and to see why, we may look in a little detail at two theologians for whom reading the Word lay at the heart of all Christian thought and speech.

[6] Ibid., p. 90.   [7] Ibid.   [8] Ibid., p. 92.   [9] Ibid., p. 91.   [10] Ibid., p. 92.
[11] On this, see my essay 'Reading Theology', *Toronto Journal of Theology* 13 (1997), pp. 53–63.
[12] Schopenhauer, *Essays and Aphorisms*, p. 93.

Calvin and Bonhoeffer

Calvin

Calvin is, of course, a scriptural rather than a speculative or systematic theologian, fulfilling his office as doctor of the church primarily through his biblical lectures, commentaries and sermons. The *Institutes* is no exception, for its purpose is, as Calvin puts it in 1559, 'to prepare and instruct candidates in sacred theology for the reading of the divine Word, in order that they may be able both to have easy access to it and to advance in it without stumbling'.[13] Much has (rightly) been made of Calvin's indebtedness to the humanist tradition, with its liberation of biblical exegesis from servility to the gloss, and of theology from servility to the sentence-method. But the principles which underlie Calvin's intense engagement with Scripture are distinctly theological: Scripture is the lode-star of his work because of what he sees as its place in the divine work of salvation, above all, its functions of announcing the gospel, reproving idolatry and fostering true piety. And there is a direct consequence here for the reading of Scripture: what is required of the reader is not simply intellectual skill, but above all a certain brokenness, from which alone truly attentive reading can follow.

In the prefatory address 'To the Reader' of a very early work, the *Psychopannychia* of 1534, Calvin gives a thumbnail sketch of the proper spiritual disposition of the reader: 'we ought to reflect that "Truth has only one voice"– that which proceeds from the lips of our Lord. To Him alone ought we to open our ears when the doctrine of Salvation is in question, while to all others we should keep our ears shut.'[14] There are some characteristic notes of what Calvin will later

---

[13] J. Calvin, 'John Calvin to the Reader', in J. T. McNeill, ed., *Institutes of the Christian Religion* (Philadelphia: Westminster Press, 1960), p. 4.

[14] J. Calvin, *Psychopannychia*, in *Tracts and Treatises*, vol. III (Edinburgh: Oliver and Boyd, 1958), p. 417.

develop: a Christological concentration on the speaking person of Christ; a stress on attentiveness; and a certain exclusivity, a refusal to give in to distraction. Calvin is particularly critical of those who are swollen with pride and so annexe Scripture to their own desires rather than submitting to its judgement. 'Is this the way of learning', he asks, 'to roll the Scriptures over and over, and twist them about in search of something that may minister to our lust, or force them into subjection to our sense?'[15] Already in this early piece Calvin is reaching towards an anthropology of the creaturely recipient of the Word in which hearing Scripture takes place as part of the conflict between desire and humility, and in which the godly reader is above all else teachable, self-mortifying and piously heedful of the Lord's voice. This is what Kort describes as 'centripetal reading':

> the act of reading Scripture involves and requires above all divestment and dislocation. A negative relation arises between the reader's world and self and the saving knowledge of God available only in and by reading Scripture, because the saving knowledge of God is not added to otherwise acquired knowledge of God, but, rather, other knowledge of God needs to be reconstituted in the light of knowledge granted in and through centripetal reading. And this displacement and re-constitution is a part of reading Scripture every time it occurs. The act of reading centripetally is inseparable from a willingness to let go of everything else, including the self, and to count all that otherwise might be thought of as good as a potential obstacle, substitute, or diversion.[16]

By the time we reach Book I of the 1559 *Institutes* Calvin has developed a rich set of reflections on many of the same themes.

Calvin's account of Scripture in Book I of the *Institutes* is part of a broader and soteriologically oriented presentation of the knowledge of God through which alone we are restored to truthful

---

[15] Ibid., pp. 417f.   [16] Kort, *'Take, Read'*, pp. 28f.

self-knowledge.[17] For Calvin, the cognitive activities of humankind
are caught up in the drama of sin and redemption: far from being
a reliable faculty or set of skills unaffected by our depravity, human
knowing is a field of vicious and wilful rejection of God – what Calvin
calls 'unrighteousness, foulness, folly, and impurity'.[18] The 'ruin of
mankind'[19] finds particularly vicious expression in *inventiveness*. At
a number of points Calvin remarks on the vile idolatry which is the
antithesis of true piety. Two instances illustrate the point:

> They do not . . . apprehend God as he offers himself, but imagine him
> as they have fashioned him in their own presumption. When this gulf
> opens, in whatever direction they move their feet, they cannot but
> plunge headlong into ruin. Indeed, whatever they afterward attempt
> by way of worship or service of God, they cannot bring as a tribute
> to him, for they are worshipping not God but a figment and a dream
> of their own heart.[20]

> [E]ach man's mind is like a labyrinth, so that it is no wonder that
> individual nations were drawn aside into various falsehoods; and
> not only this – but individual men, almost, had their own gods. For
> as rashness and superficiality are joined to ignorance and darkness,
> scarcely a single person has ever been found who did not fashion for
> himself an idol or spectre in place of God. Surely just as waters boil up

---

[17] The primacy of the theological, specifically the soteriological and revelatory, context
of Calvin's understanding of reading Scripture is seriously neglected in Kort's
presentation, which detaches what Calvin has to say about the reader from Calvin's
understanding of the nature of the biblical texts and of their function in God's
communication of himself to sinners. Hence Kort proposes that Calvin's doctrine of
Scripture 'deals, not so much with the nature of biblical texts or with their origins as
with *reading* them' ('*Take, Read*', p. 19). For Calvin, however, the practice of reading is
determined by the nature of the texts as instruments of divine speech. Kort's
misunderstanding of Calvin on this matter is to be traced to his general unease with
any appeal to transcendence, and his emphasis that the category of 'scripture' is to be
understood immanently, that is, in terms of cultural practices, and not
transcendentally (as in notions of 'canon', which Kort rejects).
[18] *Institutes of the Christian Religion* I.i.2 (p. 37).
[19] Ibid., I.ii.1 (p. 40).   [20] Ibid., I.iv.1 (pp. 47f.).

from a vast, full spring, so does an immense crowd of gods flow forth
from the human mind, while each one, in wandering about with too
much license, wrongly invents this or that about God himself.[21]

For Calvin, the counter to the vanity, instability and sheer artfulness
of the impious self is 'another and better help', namely 'the light
of his Word' by which God becomes 'known unto salvation'.[22] God
counters pride by self-revelation through Scripture. Scripture is on
Calvin's account 'a special gift, where God, to instruct the church,
not merely uses mute teachers but also opens his own most hallowed
lips. Not only does he teach the elect to look upon a god, but also
shows himself as the God upon whom they are to look.'[23] And thus:
'We must come . . . to the Word, where God is truly and vividly
described to us from his works, while these very works are appraised
not by our depraved judgement but by the rule of eternal truth.'[24]

What are the anthropological dimensions of this 'coming to the
Word' through the attestation of Scripture?

> Now, in order that true religion may shine upon us, we ought to hold
> that it must take its beginning from heavenly doctrine and that no-
> one can get even the slightest taste of right and sound doctrine unless
> he be a pupil of Scripture. Hence, there also emerges the beginning of
> true understanding when we reverently embrace what it pleases God
> there to witness of himself. But not only faith, perfect and in every
> way complete, but all right knowledge of God is born of obedience.[25]

Three things are worthy of note here. First, knowledge of God is for
Calvin antithetical to 'thinking for oneself'. 'How slippery is the fall of
the human mind into forgetfulness of God, how great the tendency to
every kind of error, how great the lust to fashion constantly new and
artificial religions', Calvin writes a few sentences further on.[26] And
so 'true religion' – that is, being bound to the truth of God – 'must
take its beginning from heavenly doctrine': God must teach. Second,

[21] Ibid., I.v.12 (pp. 64f.). [22] Ibid., I.vi.1 (pp. 69f.). [23] Ibid., I.vi.1 (p. 70).
[24] Ibid., I.vi.3 (p. 73). [25] Ibid., I.vi.2 (p. 72). [26] Ibid., I.vi.3 (p. 72).

to this divine doctrine corresponds the fact that we are 'pupils' of Scripture; neither its masters nor its critics but learners in its school. And so, third, the heart of understanding is reverence and obedience towards the divine self-witness.

The whole can be summed up with a question and answer from the earlier Geneva Catechism, which gives us an exquisitely concentrated statement of the Christian anthropology of reading Scripture:

> Q How are we to use [Scripture] in order to profit by it?
> A By receiving it with the full consent of our conscience, as truth come down from heaven, submitting ourselves to it in right obedience, loving it with a true affection by having it imprinted on our hearts, we may follow it entirely and conform ourselves to it.[27]

All that Calvin has to say is there: the insistence that right use of Scripture is for spiritual profit; the requirement for the consent of conscience (*conscience/conscientia* being, of course, not a function of deliberative acts of the human will but of the conformity of mind and will to given truth); submission, obedience and affection as primary in human reception of the Word; and, undergirding all else, a sense that encountering Scripture is encountering 'truth come down from heaven'. Nothing here suggests the absence of an anthropological component: for Calvin, there are always 'two parts', not just to the content but also to the process of knowing God and ourselves.[28] What it does suggest is that in the economy of grace the creaturely counterpart of revelation is reverent attention to that text in which God speaks 'as it were by his own mouth'.

Bonhoeffer

In interpreting Bonhoeffer's work, it is fatally easy to take insufficient account of the fact that 'most of Bonhoeffer's work is biblical

[27] *Calvin's Geneva Catechism 1541*, in T. F. Torrance, ed., *The School of Faith* (London: Clarke, 1959), pp. 52f.

[28] Cf. *Institutes* I.i.1.

exposition'[29] apart from his two dissertations *Sanctorum Communio*[30] and *Act and Being*.[31] Most students of Bonhoeffer have gravitated towards other issues: sociality and the ethical, most of all.[32] One result of this is an over-theorised picture of Bonhoeffer: the practical directness of Bonhoeffer's biblical writings and his sense that biblical exposition is a task of the theologian in which theory may be a hindrance have been lost from view.

After *Sanctorum Communio* and *Act and Being*, Bonhoeffer's interest in systematic and philosophical theology declined. As he became increasingly preoccupied with direct interpretation of Scripture, the genre of his writing shifted to something a good deal less formal and conceptual. He became, in effect, a practical, biblical theologian, writing with what is often drastic simplicity and force. The determined plainness and resistance to intellectual sophistication is to be taken at face value: to read the biblical writings from the 1930s is not to be invited to reflect, but to be summoned by evangelical address.

---

[29] E. G. Wendel, *Studien zur Homiletik Dietrich Bonhoeffers* (Tübingen: Mohr, 1985), p. 68.

[30] D. Bonhoeffer, *Sanctorum Communio. A Theological Study of the Sociology of the Church* (Minneapolis: Fortress, 1998).

[31] D. Bonhoeffer, *Act and Being. Transcendental Philosophy and Ontology in Systematic Theology* (Minneapolis: Fortress, 1996).

[32] An early important survey of the territory was offered by R. Grunow, 'Dietrich Bonhoeffers Schriftauslegung', in *Die Mündige Welt*, vol. 1 (Munich: Kaiser, 1955), pp. 62–76; Grunow did much to shape later accounts, such as that by W. Harrelson, 'Bonhoeffer and the Bible', in M. Marty, ed., *The Place of Bonhoeffer* (London: SCM, 1963), pp. 115–42. Other basic accounts of Bonhoeffer's biblical interests can be found in J. W. Woelfel, *Bonhoeffer's Theology. Classical and Revolutionary* (Nashville: Abingdon, 1970), pp. 208–38; J. A. Phillips, *The Form of Christ in the World* (London: Collins, 1967), pp. 84–105; J. D. Godsey, *The Theology of Dietrich Bonhoeffer* (London: SCM, 1960), pp. 119–94. See also the important study by M. Kuske, *The Old Testament as the Book of Christ* (Philadelphia: Westminster, 1976). Despite its declared hermeneutical interests, E. Feil's *The Theology of Dietrich Bonhoeffer* (Philadelphia: Fortress, 1985) has little to say about Scripture; F. de Lange, *Waiting on the Word. Dietrich Bonhoeffer on Speaking about God* (Grand Rapids: Eerdmans, 2000) is a highly abstract rendering of the materials which seriously misconstrues what Bonhoeffer is about.

This is why (*contra*, for example, Charles Marsh) it is entirely proper to read writings like *Life Together* or *Discipleship* as 'pietistic and naive',[33] provided that we use such terms to advertise the fact that Bonhoeffer is concerned to unleash the critical power of the scriptural word without the mediation of conceptual sophistication. To find in these homiletical writings 'important sub-textual discussions with Bonhoeffer's philosophical conversation partners' or 'an elaborate texture of biblical, philosophical and political thematics'[34] is to miss the point. The direct, homiletical rhetoric, the deliberate avoidance of technicality or complexity, the prose stripped to the basics are all tokens of the fact that Bonhoeffer has come round to an understanding of the task of interpreting Scripture which is governed by two convictions: that Holy Scripture is the *viva vox Dei*, and that this living voice demands an attitude of ready submission and active compliance.

The presupposition of the biblical writings of Bonhoeffer's middle period is that in Scripture God makes himself present in a direct way (a point easy to miss in the rather loose moralising readings of these works, especially *Life Together* and *Discipleship*). Bonhoeffer articulates that presupposition in a remarkable lecture from August 1935 on the 'Making Present of New Testament Texts'.[35] Along with Barth's much more famous riposte to Bultmann from the early 1950s, this lecture is one of the few really serious attempts to call into question on theological grounds the entire project of 'hermeneutical realisation' which has exercised such fascination for modern theology and biblical interpretation.

Bonhoeffer distinguishes two senses of *Vergegenwärtigung*. In the first sense, it is a matter of justifying the biblical message before the tribunal of the present; in the second, of justifying the present

---

[33] C. Marsh, *Reclaiming Dietrich Bonhoeffer. The Promise of his Theology* (Oxford: Oxford University Press, 1994), p. x.

[34] Ibid., pp. xf.

[35] 'Vergegenwärtigung neutestamentlicher Texte', in *Gesammelte Schriften*, vol. III (Munich: Kaiser, 1966), pp. 303–24.

before the tribunal of the biblical message. Bonhoeffer is decidedly hostile to the former sense, which he believes is trapped in a false relation to Scripture. It assumes that we have in ourselves (whether in reason, or culture, or *Volk*) 'the Archimedean point by which Scripture and proclamation are to be judged'.[36] On this, Bonhoeffer is quite blunt: 'This making present of the Christian message leads directly to paganism.'[37] Bonhoeffer is notably critical of turning the question of 'making present' into a 'methodological question', for lurking within that is a disordered relation to Scripture, indeed, 'a dangerous decadence of faith'.[38]

Such a critique emerges, however, out of a distinctive conception of the nature of Holy Scripture, one which has already moved beyond that presupposed in the exegetical work of *Creation and Fall*, above all because Bonhoeffer now assumes the perspicuity of Scripture. Scripture's perspicuity renders redundant the somewhat cumbersome technicalities of the philosophy of existence which burden the exposition of the early chapters of Genesis. What Bonhoeffer contests is the assumption that Holy Scripture is inert until realised by interpretative acts of 'making present'. 'True making present' requires no 'act of making present';[39] rather, it is a matter of 'the question of the *Sache*', of the text itself. Issues of interpretation are subservient to issues of the matter of the text, namely Jesus Christ who here announces his presence. 'When Christ comes to speech in the word of the New Testament, there is "making present". Not where the present puts forward its claim before Christ but where the present stands before Christ's claim, *there is "making present".*'[40] Whereas projects of *Vergegenwärtigung* absolutise the interpreter's present, summoning the texts before that present for review and possible 'realisation', Bonhoeffer argues that the human present is not determined by 'a definition of time'[41] but by 'the word of Christ as the Word of God'. 'The *concretissimum* of the Christian message and of the exposition

---

[36] Ibid., p. 304.   [37] Ibid., p. 305.   [38] Ibid., p. 306.   [39] Ibid.
[40] Ibid., p. 307.   [41] Ibid., p. 304.

of texts is not a human act of "making present", but is always God himself, in the Holy Spirit.'[42]

There is a direct consequence here for the task of interpretation which shapes very profoundly the biblical writings of this period of Bonhoeffer's life. Christian proclamation becomes relevant through *Sachlichkeit*, that is, though being 'bound to Scripture'.[43] The 'matter' of the New Testament is Christ present in the word; he, not I, is the proper logical subject of *Vergegenwärtigung*,[44] and so the making present of the text is nothing other than *Auslegung des Wortes*.[45] Crucially, this means that the task of establishing relevance is not pre- or post-exegetical; on the contrary, exegesis itself performs this task, and does so because the textual word which is the concern of exegesis is Christ's address to church and world in the potency of the Spirit. That word is not as it were waiting on the fringes of the human present, hoping somehow to be made real; it announces itself in its own proper communicative vigour.

In terms of our main interest in this chapter, this account of the utter concreteness of Scripture and its interpretation forms the background to the picture of the true reader of Scripture. The question of the correct attitude which the reader of Scripture is to demonstrate is an important one for Bonhoeffer. Indeed, the 'Introduction to Daily Meditation', written by Bethge under Bonhoeffer's supervision and circulated from Finkenwalde in 1936, caused Barth some unease on precisely this score. In a letter to Bonhoeffer from the Bergli on 14 October of that year, Barth wrote; 'I read it carefully but I can hardly say that I am very happy about it. I cannot go with the distinction in principle between theological work and devotional edification which is evident in this piece of writing and which I can also perceive in your letter. Furthermore, an almost indefinable odour of a monastic ethos and pathos in the former writing disturbs me.'[46] Evidently Bonhoeffer did not share Barth's fear that Finkenwalde might represent a

[42] Ibid., p. 307.   [43] Ibid.   [44] Cf. ibid., pp. 309f.
[45] Ibid., p. 308. See also 'Finkenwalder Homiletik', ibid., pp. 253f.
[46] *The Way to Freedom* (London: Collins, 1966), p. 121.

retreat from 'the original Christological-eschatological beginning in favour of some kind of realisation . . . in a specifically human sphere'.[47] Barth's fears *might* be appropriate in view of the later prison writings; but in the light of both the lecture on *Vergegenwärtigung* from the previous year and other things which Bonhoeffer has to say about the proper attitude of the biblical interpreter, Barth's unease was, at least for the moment, misplaced.

More than anything else, it is *listening* or *attention* which is most important to Bonhoeffer,[48] precisely because the self is not grounded in its own disposing of itself in the world, but grounded in the Word of Christ. Reading the Bible, as Bonhoeffer puts it in *Life Together*, is a matter of finding ourselves *extra nos* in the biblical history:

> We are uprooted from our own existence and are taken back to the holy history of God on earth. There God has dealt with us, with our needs and our sins, by means of the divine wrath and grace. What is important is not that God is a spectator and participant in our life today, but that we are attentive listeners and participants in God's action in the sacred story, the story of Christ on earth. God is with us today only as long as we are there.[49]

> Our salvation is 'from outside ourselves' (*extra nos*). I find salvation, not in my life story, but only in the story of Jesus Christ . . . What we call our life, our troubles, and our guilt is by no means the whole of reality; our life, our need, our guilt, and our deliverance are there in the Scriptures.[50]

---

[47] Ibid., p. 120.

[48] It is the 'listening self' rather than the 'worshipping self' which is basic to Bonhoeffer, *contra* D. Ford, *Self and Salvation* (Cambridge: Cambridge University Press, 1999), p. 250.

[49] *Life Together* (Minneapolis: Fortress, 1996), p. 62.

[50] Ibid. I take such remarks from Bonhoeffer as the basis for Marsh's claim that he pits 'revelation's prevenient alterity' against the 'self-constitutive subject' of modernity (Marsh, *Reclaiming Dietrich Bonhoeffer*, p. xi) – though it seems an excessively theoretical and laboured way of stating Bonhoeffer's essentially spiritual point.

This being the case, the proper reader of Scripture is not a technician; to think in such terms would be to adopt a perilously false spiritual posture. 'Proper reading of Scripture is not a technical exercise that can be learned; it is something that grows or diminishes according to my spiritual condition.'[51] We need, Bonhoeffer reminded the recipients of the 1936 circular letter on daily meditation, to 'learn the danger of escaping from meditation to biblical scholarship'.[52] Or, more pointedly: 'The Word of Scripture must never stop sounding in your ears and working in you all day long, just like the words of someone you love. And just as you do not analyse the words of someone you love, but accept them as they are said to you, accept the Word of Scripture and ponder it in your heart, as Mary did. That is all. That is meditation.'[53] The point of such remarks is not to subjectivise the Scriptures, making them into simply the occasion for charged feelings. 'Accept' is the key word. '[S]imply go and obey. Do not interpret or apply, but do it and obey. That is the only way Jesus' word is really heard', Bonhoeffer wrote in *Discipleship*.[54] A well-known letter from Bonhoeffer to his brother-in-law Rüdiger Schleicher reinforces the point: 'I want to confess quite simply that I believe the Bible alone is the answer to all our questions, and that we need only to ask persistently and with some humility in order to receive the answer from it. One simply cannot read the Bible the way one reads other books. One must be prepared to really question it. Only then will it open itself up. Only when we await the final answer from the Bible will it be given to us.'[55] The point, again, is not personalising or immanentising Scripture, drawing it into the reader's psychic sphere, or perhaps the social sphere of the meditating community. Quite the opposite: 'We will only be happy in our reading of the Bible when we dare to approach it as the means by which God really speaks to us.'[56] And grasping what is involved in that approach involves making a

---

[51] *Life Together*, p. 64.   [52] *The Way to Freedom*, p. 60.   [53] Ibid., p. 59.

[54] D. Bonhoeffer, *Discipleship* (Minneapolis: Fortress, 2001) p. 181.

[55] *Meditating on the Word* (Cambridge, Mass.: Cowley, 1986), pp. 43f.

[56] Ibid., p. 44.

sharp contrast: 'I either know about the God I seek from my own experience and insights, from the meanings which I assign to history or nature – that is, from within myself – or I know about him based on his revelation of his own Word.'[57] Moreover, what we encounter in that revelation is not some satisfying extension of our previous selves, but rather something strange and disagreeable, for 'if it is God who says where he will be, then that will truly be a place which at first sight is not agreeable to me, which does not fit so well with me. That place is the cross of Christ.'[58] In a crucial expansion of the point, Bonhoeffer writes thus:

> Does this perspective somehow make it understandable to you that I do not want to give up the Bible as this strange Word of God at any point, that I intend with all my powers to ask what God wants to say to us here? Any other place outside the Bible has become too uncertain for me. I fear that I will only encounter some divine double of myself there. Does this somehow help you to understand why I am prepared for a *sacrificium intellectus* – just in these matters, and only in these matters, with respect to the one, true God? And who does not bring to some passages his sacrifice of the intellect, in the confession that he does not yet understand this or that passage in Scripture, but is certain that even they will be revealed one day as God's own Word? I would rather make that confession than try to say according to my own opinion: this is divine, that is human.[59]

None of this, it needs to be emphasised, is a matter of abandoning the reading of Scripture to the merely affective, or of promoting ignorant or undisciplined reading. The affections are involved, but they are shaped; and what prevents ignorance and lack of discipline is not methodological rigour, but something infinitely more taxing: what Barth called the *epochē* of the interpreter in favour of the Word of the living Christ.[60]

---

[57] Ibid.   [58] Ibid., p. 45.   [59] Ibid., p. 46.
[60] Cf. K. Barth, *Church Dogmatics* 1/2 (Edinburgh: T. & T. Clark, 1956), pp. 470f.

Faithful reading in the economy of grace

With Calvin and Bonhoeffer in mind, we may turn to a dogmatic depiction of *faithful reading in the economy of grace*. The term 'reading' is chosen deliberately in preference to the term 'interpretation'. 'Reading' is a more practical, low-level term, less overlain with the complexities of hermeneutical theory, less patent of exposition through a theory of the human subject, and less likely to be overwhelmed by psychological or philosophical abstraction. Moreover, as a more modest term, 'reading' is more fitting in view of the self-presenting or self-explicating character of the divine revelation which Scripture serves.[61] The term 'interpretation', on the other hand – at least as it has been shaped in the mainstream of theological hermeneutics since Schleiermacher – tends to devote much more attention to immanent explication of the activity of the interpreting subject as that through which the text achieves its 'realisation': for this reason, 'reading' is much to be preferred. Reading Holy Scripture is 'faithful' reading: exegetical reason caught up in faith's abandonment of itself to the power of the divine Word to slay and to make alive. 'Faithful reading' takes place in the economy of grace. It is an

---

[61] Dalferth distinguishes sharply between 'hearing' and 'reading', on the grounds that reading is only a matter of 'virtual' personal encounter, whereas 'in contrast to reading, hearing necessarily has the character of actual personal interaction . . . It is tied to the communicative co-presence of persons': I. U. Dalferth, 'Von der Vieldeutigkeit der Schrift und der Eindeutigkiet des Wortes Gottes', in R. Ziegert, ed., *Die Zukunft des Schriftprinzips* (Stuttgart: Deutsche Bibelgesellschaft, 1994) p. 158. Hearing is on his account theologically and anthropologically fundamental for depiction of faith's encounter with God's self-communicative presence: 'Like the situation of Jesus' proclamation, the fundamental situation of the constitution of the Christian faith is a situation of hearing, not of reading' (ibid.). Moreover, for Dalferth 'reading' (by its emphasis on the textual character of encounter with God) tends to extract Scripture from the kerygmatic and liturgical context of the church's use, thereby turning revelation into a semantic quality of texts rather than a pragmatic reality. In its orientation to the practices of faith's encounter with the presence of God, my account of 'reading' is closely similar to Dalferth's account of 'hearing', although somewhat more objective.

intellectual activity in a determinate field or space, the space made in human time, culture and reason by God's reconciling presence as Word and Spirit. Within that space, to read Holy Scripture is to participate in the history of sin and its overcoming; to encounter the *clear* Word of God; and to be a pupil in the school of Christ.

Faithful reading of Holy Scripture in the economy of grace is an episode in the history of sin and its overcoming.

The creaturely act of reading Holy Scripture is an event in the history of God's revelatory self-giving to humankind (in this respect it is analogous to the action of 'receiving' the sacraments). As an aspect of the history of revelation, reading Scripture is equally part of the history of reconciliation, for God's communicative self-presence always takes its stand in the midst of the mind's estrangement from God. Coming to know God, and reading Holy Scripture as an aspect of this coming to know God, can only occur through the overcoming of fallenness, in the form of ignorance and idolatry. Sin as ignorance means that the saving divine address is strange to the sinner: our complicity in sin is such that the matter of the gospel which is encountered in reading Scripture is alien, incommensurable. Sin as idolatry means that as sinners we are busy with the production of images to hold down, reject or alter the matter of the gospel, so that its gracious judgement can be neutralised or averted by something of our own invention. We do not read well; and we do not read well, not only because of technical incompetence, cultural distance from the substance of the text or lack of readerly sophistication, but also and most of all because in reading Scripture we are addressed by that which runs clean counter to our will. Reading Scripture is thus a moral matter; it requires that we become certain kinds of readers, whose reading is taken up into the history of reconciliation. The separation of reason from virtue in modernity has made this acutely difficult for us to grasp. Nevertheless, a Christian theological anthropology will envisage the act of reading Scripture as an instance of the fundamental pattern of all Christian existence, which is dying and rising with Jesus Christ through the purging and quickening power of the Holy Spirit. Reading Scripture is thus best understood as an aspect of mortification and vivification: to read Scripture is to be slain and made alive. And because of this, the rectitude of the will, its conformity to the matter of the gospel, is crucial, so that reading can only occur as a kind of brokenness, a relinquishment of willed mastery of the text, and through exegetical reason's guidance towards that encounter with God of which the text is an instrument.[62]

Reading requires 'hermeneutical conversion'.[63] But a great deal of care needs to be exercised if an account of the matter is not to be ensnared in moralism. Readerly virtues are not a sphere of unaided human competence. The virtues of the godly reader through which right use is made of Scripture cannot be crafted, whether through a private process of spiritual self-cultivation or through appropriation of the habits and patterns of living which are acted out in the public life of the Christian community. Reading Scripture is an episode in the history of sin and its overcoming; and overcoming sin is the sole work of Christ and the Spirit. The once-for-all abolition and the

---

[62] One of the strengths of Wenz's fine study *Das Wort Gottes* is its insistence that the so-called 'crisis of the Scripture principle' is not only a symptom of a peculiarly modern attitude to texts and their historical character, but also and more importantly a sign of the permanent crisis in the relation of God and humankind. Scripture on this account is the site of the 'conflict between God's word and the human word. This conflict is the expression of the *eschatological power struggle between God and Anti-God for rule over humankind*' (A. Wenz, *Das Wort Gottes – Gericht und Rettung. Untersuchungen zur Autorität der Heiligen Schrift in Bekenntnis und Lehre der Kirche* (Göttingen: Vandenhoeck und Ruprecht, 1996), p. 83; see also pp. 290–2). One may wonder whether Wenz narrows matters by resolving the eschatological conflict between God and humankind into a conflict over Scripture, and whether he is therefore correct to speak of the authority of Scripture without further qualification as 'identical . . . with the authority of the triune God himself' (p. 83). But much may be learned from Wenz's avowal that problems of interpretation are inseparable from problems of authority and its repudiation, and from opposition to Scripture as an external (that is, effective and imperative, not merely suggestive) divine word.

[63] C. Rowland, 'Christology, Controversy and Apocalypse: New Testament Exegesis in the Light of the Work of William Blake', in D. G. Horrell and C. M. Tuckett, eds., *Christology, Controversy and Community* (Leiden: Brill, 2000), p. 370.

constant checking of our perverse desire to hold the text in thrall and to employ it as an extension of our will can only be achieved through an act which is not our own. The reader's will needs not simply to be called to redirect itself to appropriate ends, but to be reborn. Reading Scripture is inescapably bound to regeneration; only after a drastic reworking of spiritual psychology can the language of virtue have its place. What is therefore fundamental in giving an account of hermeneutical conversion is not a theory of moral virtue or the reader's 'character', but a soteriology and a pneumatology. Through the incarnate Word, crucified and risen, we are made capable of hearing the gospel, but only as we are at one and the same time put to death and raised to new life. Through the Spirit of the crucified and risen Christ we are given the capacity to set mind and will on the truth of the gospel and so read as those who have been reconciled to God.[64]

[64] My emphasis on the need for theological language to talk of hermeneutical conversion differs substantially from Kort's account of 'centripetal reading', which, although it is developed in conversation with Calvin, is heavily dominated by Kristeva's understanding of 'abjection' (in, for example, J. Kristeva, *Powers of Horror. An Essay on Abjection* (New York: Columbia University Press, 1982)). Kort writes: 'Reading the Bible involves first of all movement away from self and world and toward their divestment and abjection. In centripetal reading the coherences and identities of the reader's situation are dissolved, and biblical coherences and identities, rather than be appropriated, are followed as indicators of an exit and then bypassed on the way to it . . . Biblical locations, plots, characters, and theological themes, when taken as directives toward this kind of reading, are invaluable and authoritative because they clarify the act of divestment and abjection, of departure and exit, and because they ask to be left behind' (*'Take, Read'*, p. 128). The difference of this from the account offered here stems partly from direct use of Christological categories to describe what Kort describes immanently: *mortificatio* and *vivificatio*, as the extension into human life of Christ's death and resurrection by the power of the Spirit who unites the believer (and therefore the believer as reader) to Christ, are *toto caelo* different from readerly self-divestment. Furthermore, for Kort the divestment which occurs in centripetal reading involves 'the divestment not only of one's world and sense of self but of biblical worlds and identities as well' (ibid.). In effect, the cognitive content of Scripture is simply an exit sign, that which one passes on the path to radical abjection. But, once again, the mortification of the reader is unavailing unless it is occasioned and sustained by the objective and transformative reality which presents itself to the

An especially important aspect of the mortification and vivifica-tion of the reader is the discipline of what might be called 'focussed attentiveness'. The Christian act of reading Holy Scripture is to be characterised by a certain exclusiveness, a deliberate directing of at-tention to the text and an equally deliberate laying aside of other concerns. Negatively, this involves a refusal to allow the mind and the affections to be seized by other preoccupations. Reading Scripture thus involves mortification of the free-range intellect which believes itself to be at liberty to devote itself to all manner of sources of fas-cination.

To this negative, there corresponds positive attentiveness to the text. The vivification of the reader's reason involves the Spirit's gift of a measure of singularity or purity in which Scripture is not one of number of possible objects of attention, even the most impor-tant in a panoply, but the one word which is to absorb us into itself. Reading Scripture well involves submitting to the process of purifica-tion which is the readerly counterpart to the *sufficiency* of Scripture. We can, says Kierkegaard, be 'deceived by too much knowledge'.[65] One of the diseases of which the reader must be healed is that of instability, lack of exclusive concentration; and part of the reader's sanctification is ordered simplification of desire so that reading can really take place. 'Let us always hang on our Lord's lips', counsels Calvin, 'and neither add to His wisdom nor mix up with it any-thing of our own, lest like leaven it corrupt the whole mass and make even the very salt which is within us to be without savour. Let us show ourselves to be such disciples as our Lord wishes to have – poor, empty, devoid of self-wisdom; eager to learn but knowing nothing, and even wishing to know nothing but what He has taught; shunning everything of foreign growth as the deadliest poison.'[66] Thus, however important the mortification of the reader, it must

reader through the service of Holy Scripture. Without such roots in Christological and pneumatological considerations, centripetal reading remains abstract self-negation.

[65] S. Kierkegaard, *Purity of Heart is to Will One Thing* (New York: Harper, 1938), p. 204.

[66] Calvin, *Psychopannychia*, p. 418.

not be abstracted from the reader's vivification. 'Faithful reading' is characterised not only by brokenness, but also by the restoration and reconstitution of exegetical reason; to stop short of this point would be to risk denying that sin has indeed been set aside. One of the functions of a genuinely operative pneumatology in this context is to articulate grounds for the reader's *confidence* that it is possible to read Holy Scripture well – having in mind the true ends of Scripture, with false desire and distraction held in check, and with reason and spirit quickened into alertness to the speeches of God. This confidence is not the antithesis of fear and trembling: like all truthful human action, it emerges out of the fear of God. And, because it is wholly dependent upon the illumination of the Spirit, it is hesitant to trust other lights (especially its own, from which it has been set free). Yet: the Spirit has been and continues to be given to illuminate the reader, and so exegetical reason may trust the promise of Christ to lead into truth by the Spirit's presence and power. In the matter of reading Holy Scripture, too, disorder and wickedness have been overcome and reason's reconciliation to God has begun.

> Faithful reading of Holy Scripture in the economy of grace is faithful reading of the clear Word of God.

There is, as we noted at the beginning of this chapter, a creaturely act of reading: for all that it is the servant of God's merciful self-manifestation, Holy Scripture is not a declaration whose end is attained simply in its being written. Revelation engenders Scripture, and Scripture has to be read if it is to minister God's communicative presence. Reading Scripture cannot but involve the acts which are part of all reading: construing words, grasping their relationships, following a narrative or argument, and so on. The creaturely response to revelation's servant form must not be spiritualised; reading Scripture is a visible creaturely act. As Augustine is at pains to emphasise in the preface to *De doctrina christiana*, it is simply untrue that 'all worthwhile illumination of the difficulties of these texts can come by a special gift of God'.[67] But, like the church in which it takes place, the Christian act of reading Scripture has *spiritual*, not only natural, visibility. That is to say, the explication of this act requires us to invoke language about the presence and activity of God, and more particularly about the Holy Spirit. Such language is, moreover, to be treated not as a distant and essentially non-functional backdrop to much more important human undertakings. It has real work to do: the invocation of language about God in the depiction of the human act of reading Scripture is not ornamental but of the essence. However, in this context as in any other, talk of God's action does not compete with, suspend or obliterate talk of creaturely activity. Rather, it *specifies* or *determines* the character of creaturely activity by indicating that creaturely acts take place in the overarching context of the economy of salvation, and that as the acts of *creatures* they are the acts of those who are being made holy, that is, transfigured by the Holy Spirit into conformity with the dying and rising of the Son of God. It is at just this point – the theological specification of creatures and their acts – that much hermeneutical theology (like much moral theology) is decidedly attenuated, since it tends to take its bearings from accounts of human selfhood borrowed from outside Christian theology. And so, again, it is at just this point that the real dogmatic work needs to be done.

Reading in the economy of grace is not *poiesis*, but intelligence directed by and towards God's self-interpreting, perspicuous Word. Such intelligence is a particular form of creaturely activity. It involves attentiveness to that which addresses me *ab extra* and lies beyond the scope of my will and desire; it is schooled by that address; it is a mode of discipleship, and therefore of necessity involves renunciation. But none of this makes it any the less a creaturely act. It simply indicates that that to which the intellectual activity of reading directs itself is a divine Word which is not inert but rather precedes and encloses

---

[67] Augustine, *On Christian Teaching* (Oxford: Oxford University Press, 1997), preface, p. 3.

the creaturely act. The precedence of the Word over the reader is what is indicated by the concepts of Scripture as 'self-interpreting' and 'perspicuous' or 'clear'. These notions, crucially, do not eliminate the necessity of reading, making exegesis a purely 'pneumatic' activity which bypasses the processes by which written materials are appropriated. Rather, they set those acts within the domain of God's self-explication.

At one level, talk of Scripture as 'self-interpreting' or 'perspicuous' is a protest against the authority of interpretative traditions or élites. In part, therefore, the point of such talk is to defend the priority of 'original' reading over reading which is merely customary or derivative, and in one sense therefore to remove reading from under what Vatican II calls 'the watchful eye of the sacred Magisterium'.[68] But to reject the *a priori* authority of traditions of interpretation is quite different from giving free rein to the individual interpreter, making exegesis into yet another kingdom ruled by unformed intellectual conscience. Scripture is self-interpreting and perspicuous by virtue of its relation to God; its clarity is inherent, not made, whether by magisterial authorities, the scholar-prince or the pious reader. This is one of the chief reasons why, if we are properly to depict the act of reading Scripture, it is crucial that this inherent perspicuity be stated with some doctrinal precision. The clarity of Scripture is a function of its place in the divine self-demonstration, and of the Spirit's work of ordering the mind, will and affections of the reader towards what Calvin called 'heavenly doctrine'. Perspicuity only makes sense when seen in a soteriological context, that is, in relation to God's act as Word and Spirit and the creature's act of faith. Like other properties of Scripture, such as sufficiency, efficacy or perfection, clarity is not a formal or natural property of the text considered in isolation. Scripture's perspicuity is not mere verbal clarity, the clarity of 'a direct and accessible report'.[69] Materialising clarity in this way is

---

[68] Vatican II, *Dei Verbum* 23.

[69] G. C. Berkouwer, *Holy Scripture* (Grand Rapids: Eerdmans, 1975), p. 270.

simply 'attributing to the book what is the gift of God'.[70] Rather, Scripture is clear because through the Spirit the text serves God's self-presentation. Properly speaking, it is not Scripture which is self-interpreting but *God* who as Word interprets himself through the Spirit's work.[71]

Because of this, perspicuity is not to be thought of as in any simple way a property of Scripture antecedent to acts of reading. Scripture is clear because of the Spirit's work in which creaturely acts of reading are so ordered towards faithful attention to the divine Word that through Scripture the light of the gospel shines in its own inherent splendour. Perspicuity is thus not a way of suggesting that reading is superfluous; it is about the way in which faithful reading within the economy of revelatory grace is not sheerly spontaneous but a receptive act of the intelligence of faith. Clarity is given, not the product of unaided exegetical prowess or technique. But it is not given as a *qualitas* of the text *ante usum*. The Holy Spirit rules, accompanies and sanctifies the work of the reader in engaging the sanctified and inspired text. This work of the reader involves, of course, the exercise of 'natural' capacities and skills. Yet the mere technical deployment of these skills is insufficient, and may, indeed, mislead. Their effective use – that is, their use towards the end of Scripture, which is attention to God – depends upon their integration into a Spirit-produced disposition on the part of the reader. Such a disposition is characterised above all by humble dependence upon God and receptivity to the teaching of the gospel. 'It is . . . necessary above all else to be moved by the fear of God towards learning his will: what it is that he instructs us to seek or avoid . . . After that it is necessary, through holiness, to become docile, and not contradict holy scripture.'[72] There is thus a direct correlation between the clarity of Scripture and the *pius lector*: clarity and holiness belong together.

[70] H. Heppe, *Reformed Dogmatics* (London: George Allen and Unwin, 1950), p. 32.

[71] Further on theological explication of *claritas scripturae*, see again Wenz, *Das Wort Gottes*.

[72] Augustine, *On Christian Teaching* II.16f. (pp. 33f.).

In sum: Scripture's clarity is neither an intrinsic element of the text as text nor simply a fruit of exegetical labour; it is that which the text *becomes* as it functions in the Spirit-governed encounter between the self-presenting saviour and the faithful reader. To read is to be caught up by the truth-bestowing Spirit of God.

This account of the clarity of Scripture in relation to acts of reading may help us reach some judgements about recent proposals concerning the role of the reader in co-constituting the text's meaning through acts of interpreting. A first example is the sophisticated work of Werner Jeanrond in *Text and Interpretation*[73] and *Theological Hermeneutics*.[74] The latter work opens with the proposal that 'text-understanding always demands our active participation in recreating the text in question. It demands that we lend our reality to the text so that it can become real for us.'[75] That is, although 'interaction between reader and text receives its energy from the continuous "provocation" of the reader by the text', nevertheless '[t]hat a text can provoke a reader is ... possible only because of the prior consent by the reader to engage in such an interaction with it'.[76] Already the basic motif can be discerned: the reader is the agent of the text's 're-alisation', and no language about (for example) Word or Spirit seems to be required, for the text's reality is borrowed from or bestowed by its reader. In *Text and Interpretation*, the reader's activity is similarly described: 'a text has an identity which, from the point of view of its design, is never purely, univocally and objectively comprehensible but is rather in constant need of an individual reading act in order for it to present itself ... reading is always ... a projection of a new image of reality, as this is co-initiated by the text and achieved by the reader in the relationship with the text in the act of reading'.[77] Though Jeanrond clearly sets some distance between himself and more

---

[73] W. Jeanrond, *Text and Interpretation as Categories of Theological Thinking* (Dublin: Gill and Macmillan, 1988).

[74] W. Jeanrond, *Theological Hermeneutics. Development and Significance* (London: SCM, 1988).

[75] Ibid., p. 1.   [76] Ibid., pp. 6f.   [77] Jeanrond, *Text and Interpretation*, p. 104.

radical theorists who deny any regulative function or determinacy to the text, he nevertheless makes the text's *Sinngestalt* (semantic form) a function of cooperation between text and reader: 'Text composition is the procedure which forms a text as a semantic potential, and reading is the procedure which realises a written text as a form of sense.'[78] The anthropology of reading here, we note, is one in which the move from semantic potentiality to semantic actuality is the reader's work. Jeanrond is, of course, in one sense correct to stress that the text is 'unrealised' before it is read, *ante usum*. However, the agent of the passage from potentiality to actuality is for Jeanrond the human reader, and the depiction of the reader does not require language about revelation, Word, Spirit or faith. The dynamic of reading is that of the immanent world of reader and text, and in such an account the 'self-interpreting' character of the text (its service, that is, of God's self-explication) has little place.

Talk of Scripture's clarity sets the act of reading in the context of Word and its anthropological correlate, faith. In this connection, mention may be made of Garrett Green's analysis of imagination in two studies, *Imagining God*[79] and, more recently, *Theology, Hermeneutics and Imagination*.[80] The earlier study offers an account of Scripture as a text through which God forms, enables and stimulates Christian imagination. 'The Christian claim that the Bible is inspired by God means that it is the instrument of revelation, the means by which God makes himself known in the present life of believers. This claim can be stated more precisely by saying that scripture embodies the paradigm through which Christians view the world in its essential relation to God, the images by which God informs the imagination of believers.'[81] Clearly on this account there

---

[78] Ibid., p. 83.

[79] G. Green, *Imagining God. Theology and the Religious Imagination* (San Francisco: Harper and Row, 1989).

[80] G. Green, *Theology, Hermeneutics and Imagination. The Crisis of Interpretation at the End of Modernity* (Cambridge: Cambridge University Press, 2000).

[81] Green, *Imagining God*, p. 108.

is need to talk of God's action through Scripture, and in this Green's work shows itself to be doctrinally better ordered than those accounts which do not go beyond ecclesial or anthropological immanence. Yet if the notion of imagination is probed, we find that it tends to give considerable importance to the human work of construing the world on the basis of the paradigms offered by Scripture. This can readily be seen in Green's account of biblical inspiration, which, he argues, '[i]s most adequately understood as [Scripture's] imaginative force'.[82] Or again, biblical authority 'is imaginative', that is, 'scripture, rightly employed, enables its readers to imagine God'.[83] Scripture is here understood as an instrument of revelation in the sense that it furnishes the reason, the capacity and the raw material for the *work* of Christian imagining. But what is lacking is a closer theological specification of this work – above all, specification of its proper self-forgetfulness, its chastened horror at its own idolatries, its reference to the work of Word and Spirit. Without these specifications, 'imagination' shares something of the fate of 'reading' in Jeanrond's hermeneutics: too much space is given to the interpreting agent, too little space to the self-presentation of God in the economy of *grace*.[84]

These problems become somewhat more pressing in Green's most recent work *Theology, Hermeneutics and Imagination.* One of the primary principles of the study is the *Bedeutungsbedürftigkeit* of all reality – the fact that everything stands in need of interpretation (the term derives from Hamann). As Green uses the term, it seems to suggest that reality (including textual reality) comes to be 'alive' through interpreting activities, and those interpreting activities find their summation in the work of imagination:

> For the believer the only way to have the world – to apprehend it Christianly – is to imagine it according to the paradigm rendered in its classic shape by the canon of scripture . . . If the meaning of

[82] Ibid., p. 112.   [83] Ibid., p. 119.

[84] Cf. here Kort, '*Take, Read*', pp. 122f., who similarly criticises Green for excessive emphasis on the perspective and practices of communities of interpretation.

the text is always open ended, it follows that there can be no escape from interpretation, and interpretation requires the active engagement of the imagination. The meaning of scripture is never simply given; it is always the fruit of an interpretative act. The inescapability of interpretation implies the hermeneutic imperative. For those who seek to live by the Bible – that is, to read the Bible scripturally – interpretation is not an optional or auxiliary activity but rather the very essence of the matter. To read the Bible as scripture *is* to interpret it.[85]

The theological grounds adduced for this are as follows:

The Lord God has created a world, so say the biblical witnesses, that is an enigma, a surd, apart from its divine origin and destiny. Seen in its godly relationship, the world does not become comprehensible so much as interpretable. It remains mysterious without being meaningless. Indeed, its meaning depends on the divine mystery at its heart, so that its meaning is not a given but is rather a task, a quest . . . The important point is that mystery . . . is not an unfortunate problem or limitation; rather, it is the chief motivator of creaturely inquiry and meditation.[86]

By way of response we may ask, first, whether this doctrine of God as mystery gives sufficient account of God's trinitarian self-presence. Green certainly affirms that God is 'the living God, a free agent who cannot be manipulated or treated as a mere object'.[87] But in the absence of trinitarian language of Word and Spirit, God's presence and human action seem to be related as *mystery* and *interpretation, motivator* and *agent*: 'The inevitability of interpretation is the hermeneutical consequence of the mystery of God.'[88] Second, we may ask whether this rather slender doctrine of God as mystery yields an account of reading Scripture in which the text – because it is not a field of divine activity – is not the clear Word of God which *makes sense*

[85] Ibid., pp. 175f.   [86] Ibid., p. 184.   [87] Ibid., p. 176.   [88] Ibid., p. 177.

and is, therefore, to be received in the humility of faith, but rather an opportunity for *making sense* through imagination. And this is another way of asking whether on Green's account Scripture is, in fact, self-interpreting, and whether imagination would be better replaced by faith as the reader's primary act.

Similar difficulties attend James K. A. Smith's recent study *The Fall of Interpretation*, which, though it approaches matters from a rather different set of doctrinal commitments, gives the same profile to the act of interpretation as does Green. Smith charges mainstream Western Protestant divinity with espousing the myth of hermeneutical immediacy. In this myth, interpretation is a post-lapsarian condition, the fruit of the fall 'from the intelligible to the sensible, from immediacy to mediation, from reading to hermeneutics'.[89] 'Eden . . . was a paradise of perpetual connection: a hermeneutical paradise precisely because of the absence of interpretation . . . Hermeneutics is a curse, but it is one from which we can be redeemed in the here and now; we can return from mediation to immediacy, from distortion to "perfect clarity", and from interpretation to "pure reading".'[90] On Smith's account, this longing for immediacy is symptomatic of a deep doctrinal disarray in the Western tradition, namely 'a devaluation of creation' which expresses itself as a 'penchant for overcoming historical and linguistic conditioning' or as the 'attempt to overcome our humanity'.[91] Smith's counter-proposal is what he calls 'a *creational model* of interpretation' which 'understands interpretation and hermeneutical mediation as constitutive aspects of human being-in-the-world'.[92]

There are surely historical problems here: the generalised charge of 'Neo-Platonism (or gnosticism)'[93] can scarcely be supported without much more rigorous demonstration. But the more serious difficulties are doctrinal. Smith's critique of the commitment to 'immediacy' which he believes is embedded in Western theological hermeneutics

[89] James K. A. Smith, *The Fall of Interpretation. Philosophical Foundations for a Creational Hermeneutic* (Downers Grove: InterVasity Press, 200), p. 17.
[90] Ibid., pp. 37f.   [91] Ibid., p. 40.   [92] Ibid., p. 22.   [93] Ibid., p. 134.

ignores the revelational and pneumatological dimensions of the notion of Scripture's *claritas*, assuming that *claritas* can be understood
simply as a text-property without the Spirit's work, or as a kind of
hermeneutical equivalent of an overly-realised eschatology. Furthermore, the book's handling of the category of 'creation' is problematic.
First, as Smith expounds it, it has a distinctly anthropological orientation: 'creation' is a way of valuing embodiment, finitude, being-in-
the-world. Second, therefore, createdness is expounded philosophically, rather than theologically, with little reference to the creature's
dependence upon the continuing presence and activity of the triune God. Third, given the frank Arminian bent of Smith's doctrinal
framework,[94] somewhat uneasily wedded to Kuyper and Dooyeweerd
(not, note, Bavinck!), the human work of interpretation threatens to
float free from talk of divine action, and the myth of immediacy is
countered by a sort of hermeneutical Pelagianism.

Finally, mention should be made of one of the very few recent
attempts to offer a theological account of reading, Klaas Huizing's
Homo legens. Huizing reconceives the Protestant Scripture-principle
from the perspective of the reader (in a way which parallels Law's
reconception of the doctrine of biblical inspiration), proposing 'theology of Scripture as theology of reading'.[95] This involves, on the
one hand, a (Derridean) rejection of 'the book' as hopelessly entangled in the identity metaphysics of onto-theology, and, on the other
hand, an exposition of the Scripture-principle which makes the centre of that doctrine the affections of the reader. 'Affective conformity
to Scripture'[96] in effect replaces the doctrines of revelation or inspiration: the status of the biblical text is determined on the basis
of its function as 'prototype', its provocation of the reader's moral
or affective life. What is alarming here is the way in which the real
work is undertaken by the reader: resurrection and Spirit (and the
corollary of Scripture's perspicuity) do not feature. Huizing certainly
speaks of the reader's encounter with an 'intentionality' other than

[94] See ibid., p. 136.   [95] Huizing, *Homo legens*, p. VII.   [96] Ibid., p. 48.

the reader's own; but it is what he calls an 'affective intentionality of Scripture',[97] an intentionality of 'the Christ who is incarnated in Scripture'.[98] Through reading, the reader is transformed into the image of Christ, the very openness of the scriptural portrayal of Christ pressing for some realisation in the life of the believer. Reading, in effect, assumes the role of the Spirit in application.

By way of contrast: 'In fact, if Scripture as testimony to Jesus Christ is the Word of God . . . who then can expound Scripture but God himself? And what can man's exposition of it consist in but once more in an act of service, a faithful and attentive following after the exposition which Scripture desires to give to itself, which Jesus Christ as Lord of Scripture wishes to give to Himself?'[99]

Such problems (which are fairly widespread in modern hermeneutical writing) could be avoided relatively easily if discussion of reading were lodged in a different doctrinal context, namely in theological affirmations about the communicative activity of God, served by the sanctified text which, as the field of the Spirit's working, is *clear*. Human acts of reading or interpretation could then be fittingly related to the divine revelatory work and presence, resulting in a more modest anthropology of reading which did not threaten to annexe to itself the Spirit's work.

Faithful reading of Holy Scripture in the economy of grace is not the work of masters but of pupils in the school of Christ.

One of the chief fruits of the Spirit's conversion of the reader is *teachableness*, a teachableness which extends into the disposition with which Scripture is read. To read Scripture as one caught up by the reconciling work of God is to abandon mastery of the text, and, instead, to be schooled into docility. In his 1522 tract 'On the Clarity and Certainty or Power of the Word of God', Zwingli writes thus:

[97] Ibid., p. 8.   [98] Ibid., p. 9.
[99] K. Barth, *The Knowledge of God and the Service of God According to the Teaching of the Reformation* (London: Hodder and Stoughton, 1938), pp. 180f.

I know for certain that God teaches me, because I have experienced it: and to prevent misunderstanding, this is what I mean when I say that I know for certain that God teaches me. When I was younger, I gave myself overmuch to human teaching, like others of my day, and when about seven or eight years ago I undertook to devote myself entirely to the Scriptures I was always prevented by philosophy and theology. But eventually I came to the point where led by the Word and Spirit of God I saw the need to set aside all these things and to learn the doctrine of God direct from His own Word. Then I began to ask God for light and the Scriptures became far clearer to me . . . than if I had studied many commentators and expositors. Note that it is always a sure sign of God's leading, for I could never have reached that point by my own feeble understanding.[100]

The thrust of this passage is not only to draw a familiar early Reformation contrast between an oppressive interpretative tradition and the clarity and vividness of 'direct', unmediated reading of Scripture. It is also to describe a proper 'spirituality' of reading, best depicted in predominantly passive terms: being led by Word and Spirit, learning the doctrine of God, asking God for light, above all, being taught. For Zwingli, to speak of God as teacher is to oppose the idolatrous effect of self-derived wisdom. 'You will not leave your human understanding', Zwingli says, 'but would rather shape the divine understanding to it . . . You would teach God and force him according to your own desires.'[101] For Zwingli, then, the real nature of the interpretative situation is best described as a struggle to replace mastery by teachableness:

The will of God is this, that he alone should be the teacher. And I intend to be taught by him and not by men . . . For it is not for us to

---

[100] H. Zwingli, *On the Clarity and Certainty or Power of the Word of God*, in G. W. Bromiley, ed., *Zwingli and Bullinger* (Philadelphia: Westminster Press, 1953), pp. 90f.
[101] Ibid., p. 91.

sit in judgement on Scripture and divine truth, but to let God do his work in and through it, for it is something which we can learn only of God. Of course, we have to give an account of our understanding of Scripture, but not in such a way that it is forced or wrested according to our own will, but rather so that we are taught by Scripture: and that is my own intention.[102]

It is from this standpoint that we may broach the question of the role of critical methods in reading Scripture. One of the main reasons why the kind of disposition recommended by Zwingli seems strange to us is the remarkable authority enjoyed by the 'critical' attitude to Scripture, and the prestige which consequently attaches to those methods which both flow from and reinforce such an attitude. Though teachableness and naiveté may be allowed to be appropriate in informal reading, they are generally considered ill-adapted for the critical task, since that task can be undertaken responsibly only if the reader thinks *about* the text, not *with* or *under* the text. The set of problems touched upon here concerns much more than the utility or otherwise of particular exegetical methods, which are only elements of larger interpretative strategies, and so only symptomatic of the deeper issues. More than anything else, we need a theological analysis of what James Barr rightly identifies as the crucial issue, namely the 'spiritual and intellectual basis of modern biblical research'.[103] Taken on its own, discussion of critical methods does not advance matters very far; much more is to be gained from unearthing the overall construal of the nature and purpose of reading within which critical methods have their place. Judgements about the appropriateness of methods rest upon prior judgements about the ends of interpretation, the proper social and institutional location of interpretation, and the proper dispositions of interpreters. In our present context, it is this last element which is particularly appropriate.

---

[102] Ibid., p. 92.
[103] See J. Barr, *Holy Scripture. Canon, Authority, Criticism* (Oxford: Clarendon Press, 1983), pp. 105–26.

The prestige of critical methods in reading biblical texts is often considered an authentic part of the heritage of the Reformation – whether as an expression of the freedom of the conscientious exegete from magisterial control (James Barr) or as the outworking in the intellectual sphere of the principle of *sola fide* with its repudiation of contingent securities (Bultmann, Ebeling). There is some historical sleight of hand here, as well as a collapsing together of Luther's understanding of Christian liberty and Kant's understanding of free inquiry. But there is a more pervasive problem, namely the way in which, when annexed to some conventions about the nature of intellectual responsibility and self-determination, critical methods can generate what by theological standards is a false stance towards Scripture as a field of divine self-communication. There is, in other words, an anthropological problem to be noted, one which concerns the way in which an intellectual activity such as reading is understood. At the heart of that problem is a sense – often implicit but nevertheless real – of the sublimity of reason, expressed as a competence and adequacy, for which the term 'mastery' is hardly too strong,[104] and which is quite antithetical to what we find in Zwingli. George Grant spoke of this in (Heideggerian) terms as the 'commanding' or 'representing' function of reason in modern ideals of technical scholarly work.[105] Both commanding and representing distance the inquirer from the matter of inquiry. When it emerges in the reading of Scripture, this distance takes the form of the assumption that in transcending the text, the professional interpreter transcends the event of God's self-communication, and so is not part of the same spiritual economy

---

[104] Whatever hesitations one might have about the critiques of intellectual institutions which derive from Nietzsche, their exposé of intellectual command is surely correct. See, for example, P. Bové, *Intellectuals in Power* (New York: Columbia University Press, 1986); P. Bové, *Mastering Discourse* (Durham, N.C.: Duke University Press, 1992); J.-F. Lyotard, *The Postmodern Condition* (Manchester: Manchester University Press, 1986).

[105] See, for example, *Technology and Justice* (Notre Dame: University of Notre Dame Press, 1986), pp. 35–77, 97–102.

as church and Scripture.[106] But to read in such a way is not to read Scripture in the economy of grace, and so not to read as learner.

This does *not* entail wholesale abandonment of any appropriation of the tools of historical inquiry, but raises a question about their usefulness by asking whether they can foster *childlike* reading of the text. In the hermetic closing pages of *Act and Being*, Bonhoeffer remarks that 'the child poses the problem of theology'.[107] By this, he means that the child figures to us something fundamental to faith, namely orientation upon Christ 'without reflection,'[108] which Bonhoeffer thinks of as an eschatological determination of human life and activity. The child images *fides directa*, a term used in Protestant orthodoxy for faith's objective (rather than reflexive) orientation. And hence '[t]he child is near to what is of the future – the *eschata*. This too is conceivable only to the faith that suspends itself before revelation.'[109] As we have already seen, a few years after writing *Act and Being* Bonhoeffer worked out its hermeneutical entailments by urging a childlike naiveté in reading Scripture. Not the least of what may be gleaned from Bonhoeffer is the lesson that reason – including exegetical reason – finds its end, not in subjecting the world to its expert gaze, but in unskilled deference to the divine teacher.

A theology of the nature of reading Scripture such as has been outlined here cannot pretend to solve exegetical problems, any more than a dogmatic moral psychology can pretend to offer solutions to ethical quandaries. An account of what makes a person good in whatever sphere of human action will not instruct us with any directness how such a person is to act in any given circumstance. But this recognition does not undermine the usefulness of dogmatic anthropology, whether in morals or hermeneutics; it simply specifies the task which such an anthropology is intended to perform. A theological

---

[106] This is brilliantly exposed in R. Jenson, 'Hermeneutics and the Life of the Church', in C. Braaten and R. Jenson, eds., *Reclaiming the Bible for the Church* (Grand Rapids: Eerdmans, 1995), pp. 89–105.

[107] *Act and Being* (London: Collins, 1961), p. 182 (here I follow the older translation).

[108] *Act and Being* (Minneapolis: Fortress, 1996), p. 157.   [109] Ibid., p. 160.

anthropology of the reader may not of itself deliver us from the struggle to make sense. But what it may do is indicate the character and end of exegetical activity, and the field in which it takes place. And more: it may suggest that a reading strategy dominated by exegetical aporias – which proceeds as if sense can only be *made* – is one which already places the exegete in a disturbed relation to the text, one in which the clarity of Scripture as divine self-communication has to prove itself by being demonstrated through the solution of accumulated problems of exegesis. And last: it may suggest that, however genuine they may be, exegetical difficulties are, in the end, not the heart of the difficulty in reading Scripture. The real problems lie elsewhere, in our defiance of grace.

4 | Scripture, Theology and the Theological School

In the autumn of 1558, Zacharius Ursinus,[1] then aged twenty-four, moved to Breslau to take up a post at the Elisabeth-Schule, teaching Latin and instructing his pupils in the basics of theology by expounding a little work from the pen of his mentor Melanchthon, the *Examen ordinandorum*. Ursinus is chiefly remembered for his place in the consolidation of Reformation theology and church life in the Palatinate under Elector Frederick III; above all, of course, he played a key role in drafting that exquisite statement of moderate Reformed teaching, the Heidelberg Catechism. More generally, he is considered a formative figure in the development of Reformed covenant theology. Although the two years which Ursinus spent teaching in Breslau are usually passed over quickly in accounts of his work, one important text from that period has come down to us, a text which is extraordinarily enlightening about the theme of this chapter, namely the relation of Holy Scripture to Christian doctrine. The text is Ursinus' 'Hortatory Oration to the Study of Divinity', his inaugural address at the Elisabeth-Schule, in which he gives an account of his understanding of the tasks of doctrine and catechesis in the congregation.[2] The hand of Melanchthon is evident throughout the oration; but

[1] On Ursinus in general, see D. Visser, *Zacharius Ursinus. The Reluctant Reformer. His Life and Times* (New York: United Church Press, 1983); K. Sudhoff, *C. Olevianus und Z. Ursinus. Leben und ausgewählte Schriften* (Elberfeld: Friedrichs, 1857).

[2] Ursinus, *Paraenesis ad theologiae et doctrinae Catecheticae sedulum studium*, in *Opera theologica*, ed. Q. Reuter (Heidelberg: Lancellot, 1612), vol. I, cols. 2–9; I follow the English translation, 'Ursine's Hortatory Oration to the Study of Divinity, together with the manifold use of Catechisme', in *The Summe of the Christian Religion, Delivered by Zacharius Ursinus . . . First Englished by D. Henry Parry* (London: 1645), pp. 1–13 (cited

whatever detailed conclusions may be reached about its authorship, the text remains a fascinating articulation of an understanding of the nature and ends of Christian theology, an account of the matter which, moreover, has been almost entirely eclipsed in the modern theological academy. My suggestion here is that it still has much to commend it, and that its sheer difference from modern conventions about the nature of theological study may press us to critical reflection upon the assumptions under which we operate. In particular, it may lead us to rearticulate the centrality of Holy Scripture to the entire enterprise of Christian theology, to question the propriety of the normative modern four-fold disciplinary arrangement of the subject, and to reinvest in the priority of theology's practical and exegetical tasks in an account of the nature and ends of the church's theology. In short: it may help identify the need to reintegrate theology with church and Word, and thereby help us consider the operations of reason in the sphere of reconciliation, and the institutional forms in which such operations may more effectively be fostered.

'A Hortatory Oration to the Study of Divinity'

In his 'Oration', Ursinus offers a defence of the necessity and utility of catechising as part of the church's task of edification through instruction, and a brief account of catechetical method. Set out in skeleton form, his argument is this: although in matters of the knowledge of God all are unskilled and infantile, and so dependent upon the revelatory work of God in Christ and Spirit in the sphere of the church congregation, the growth in godliness which God requires of believers does not take place independently of instruction in Christian doctrine. Doctrine is the means through which Christ builds up the church as his kingdom, and so teaching is essential

as 'Oration'). The circumstances of the *Antrittsrede* are usefully set out in E. K. Sturm, *Der junge Zacharius Ursin. Sein Weg vom Philippismus zum Calvinismus* (Neukirchen: Neukirchener Verlag, 1972), pp. 111–23.

to Christian edification. The catechetical method offers a primary instrument for laying out Christian doctrine in a suitable fashion for those growing in faith, offering a summary of biblical teaching in brief compass. Over against the Schwenkfeldian fanatics,[3] who contend that God communicates without the offices of teaching and study, Ursinus commends the importance of the orderly life of the school and its patterns of instruction as the means used by God to bestow understanding of prophetic and apostolic truth.

In essence, the 'Oration' is a commendation of the role of doctrine in the building up of the church, and of the school as the form of common life in which doctrine can be transmitted and Christian nurture fostered. For our present purposes, what is most interesting, as well as most disconcerting, about what Ursinus has to say is his assumption about the primacy of Holy Scripture, both for the whole of theology and for the entire life of the theological school. At the heart of Ursinus' vision of theology and the form of common life in which it may flourish is the lively self-exposition of the Word.

Scripture and doctrine

Christian doctrine, Ursinus announces at the beginning of his 'Oration', 'is a doctrine which (I say) not only is still unknowne to the wisest and most sharp-witted of men, unless they be taught by the voice of the Church, and efficacy of the Spirit; but also in a great part was unknown to the Angels themselves before it was disclosed by the

---

[3] Behind Ursinus' critique of 'fanaticall minded men' who are suborned by Satan to propose that 'God communicates himself to us immediately' ('Oration', p. 4) lies the 1554 debate of Melachthon and Hyperius with Schwenkfeld, who had denied the mediated character of God's self-communication. God, Schwenkfeld argued, 'wirckt nit durch mittel der creaturen in der seele sonder durch den einigen Mitler sinen son Jesum Christum'; God 'bedarf keines creaturlichen mitels noch instruments oder werckzeügs zu seinen götlichen hendeln': Schwenkfeld, 'Verantwortung vnd gegenbericht' [1554] in D. Hartranft et al, eds., *Corpus Schwenkfeldianorum* (Leipzig: 1907–61), vol. XIII, p. 987.

Son, from the secret bosome of his eternall Father'.[4] From the beginning, that is, Ursinus is concerned to advance a two-fold argument:
doctrine transcends human intellectual capacity; yet, by the promise
and command of God, Christian truth can be both taught and learned
in the church. As a human undertaking, *doctrina* (by which Ursinus
means both the content of Christian instruction and the processes of
teaching and being taught) simply exceeds human ability: it is divine
truth 'which to unfold and praise, if men and Angels should bend
all the strength of wit and eloquence, yet were they never able to
speak of it, according to the due compasse and worth of the thing'.[5]
And so Ursinus approaches his task in the school with apprehension,
fearful of 'how much I might sinke under this charge'.[6] As much as
their charges, teachers themselves are 'children, not only in regard of
age, but also in regard of understanding, or performance of any action', for 'all who do meditate or speak anything concerning God' are
'infants in understanding and utterance, touching all matters divine'.[7]
Crucially, however, for Ursinus the weakness of teachers and learners
is the obverse of the fact that God fosters the learning of Christian
doctrine through frail instruments. 'God', he says, 'will be effectual
by weak and abject meanes; according to that of the Psalmist, *Out of
the mouthes of babes and sucklings hast thou ordained strength.*'[8]

 We can, perhaps, already begin to identify the deep divide between Ursinus' assumptions about the nature and task of theology
and those with which we are familiar in much modern academic
work in the discipline. Faced with Ursinus' realisation of the transcendence of the matter of theology (the knowledge of God), modern
instincts school us to interpret the attendant difficulty as a signal of
the unavailability of God for reason's comprehension, and so to retreat into agnostic silence, or perhaps to change tack and, instead of
investigating God, to investigate religion and its conditions. For Ursinus, on the other hand, matters are very different: his account of the
matter presumes that theology is not in a situation in which whatever

---

[4] 'Oration', p. 1.   [5] Ibid.   [6] Ibid.   [7] Ibid., pp. 1f.   [8] Ibid., p. 1.

eludes our intellectual grasp must remain for ever beyond us. Our incapacity to speak of 'the compasse and worth of the thing' is not final, because it is countered by a movement from God towards us, overruling our inability and making fitting speech possible. Doctrine is indeed 'unknowne to the wisest, and most sharp-witted of men, unlesse they be taught by the voice of the Church, and efficacy of the Spirit'. The word 'unlesse' there is crucial: Ursinus is resisting the sceptical impulse by invoking language about God's revelatory presence and activity in the church, confident that such language is more than adequate compensation for human ineptitude. The key is thus to envisage the activity of theology as taking place in a trinitarian, soteriological and ecclesial context – in what we have earlier referred to as the economy of grace. 'In this businesse of maine importance, God useth our infancy to illustrate his glory; the greatnes of the work, and weaknes of the instrument plainly proving, that so great a matter is not effected or dependent by and on our, but God's effectuall power.'[9]

Three corollaries are drawn from this. The first is that the theological teacher is an office-holder, and thereby in receipt of a promise of divine assistance. '[W]hen I well weigh the nature of mine office, I perceive I ought with all cheerfulness . . . [to] obey God that calls me to so honourable an imployment; especially he promising mee assistance, with which whosoever are assisted, may despaire in nothing.'[10] Theological activity, that is, is neither spontaneous nor autonomous. Ursinus' model theological teacher is very far from the critical hero of Kant's *Conflict of the Faculties*, being subject to the divine calling and therefore a recipient of the divine aid. The second corollary is that the end of the teaching and learning of doctrine is edification of the church. By the mouths of infants, Ursinus argues, the Lord (in the psalmist's words) 'founds a kingdom'. 'Hee speaketh of the strength or kingdome, which is seen in this life, called the kingdome of Christ: which is, the Son of God instituting and preserving of a

---

[9] Ibid., p. 3.   [10] Ibid., p. 1.

ministery, thereby gathering a Church, quickning beleevers by the sound of the Gospel, and sanctifying them by the holy Spirit to eternall life, defending the Church in this life against the kingdome of the Divell, and after this life raising them up holy to eternall life; that in them may reign the Godhead evidently, and not covertly by the ministery.'[11] Doctrine is critical for the coherence and grounding of the church, for 'as good laws are the sinews of a politicall kingdom: so this kingdom is gathered, kept, and governed, by the doctrine concerning Christ. And as without a foundation the building cannot consist: so unlesse we hold to Christ, and what he is, and what he hath done for us, whatsoever else may seem to be piety or comfort, it's fading, it's feigned, it's nothing.'[12] Because the end of doctrine is nurture, there is for Ursinus no distance between the theological teacher and the church: called by God, the teacher's self-understanding is derived from his place in the community as Christ's kingdom, and the teacher's activity directed solely to its flourishing. Third, and most important here, is the centrality of Holy Scripture for the entire process of teaching and learning of doctrine. '[A]s the babe grows not to ripenesse of man-hood, unlesse he be fed with the mother's milk, or convenient food: so we likewise, that we may not fail of our hoped perfection, ought not to refuse the *milk of the Word*, whereby we are nourished and suckled to eternal life.'[13] Teaching and learning are required, therefore, not as speculative activities but as engagement with the 'rudiments, which to reason are hidden wisdome, [and] are both necessary and sufficient to everlasting salvation'.[14] With this we move to look more directly at the place of Scripture in the 'Oration'.

Scripture and catechesis

Ursinus explains his understanding of catechesis by offering a gloss on the phrase in 2 Tim. 1.13 concerning 'the pattern of the sound words' which Timothy has heard from Paul. He comments: 'The Apostle

[11] Ibid., p. 2.   [12] Ibid.   [13] Ibid.   [14] Ibid.

meaning a draught or plat-forme of sound positions, concerning each point of doctrine, methodically and briefly comprised, as if it were painted before the eye, together with a kinde and manner of teaching and expression, as is both proper, plain, and agreeable with the stile of the Prophets and Apostles'.[15] Though Ursinus' chief concern is the nature of the catechism, four matters of more general significance for our understanding of Christian theology may be drawn from this brief definition.

First, theology is a 'draught or plat-forme', a sketch or outline of the elements of Christian teaching (Ursinus Latinises ὑποτύπωσις from 2 Tim. 1.13). What surfaces there is the same lightweight and unsystematic understanding of theology that we find in Calvin's *Institutes* and Melanchthon's *Loci communes*. The task of catechesis and hence of theology is not one of systematic reformulation and representation of the Christian faith, or of offering a better-warranted, more orderly and precise account of Christian teaching than is found in the everyday speech of the church's life and ministry. Rather, all that theology offers is a simple sketch or outline of the different parts of Christian teaching with an eye to their scope and interrelations. There is no organising principle, whether doctrinal, philosophical or experiential; no prolegomena; and no interest in defence or apologetic commendation: the aim is simple summary description.[16] Because of this, second, there is only quite minimal organisation of the

---

[15] Ibid., p. 4.

[16] The catechetical aspect of Ursinus' work is thus not easy to reconcile with the view that his theology indicates a shift into a scholastic register. Thus John Platt argues that 'with Ursinus the philosophical arguments for God's existence achieve a status hitherto unknown in Reformation theology': J. Platt, *Reformed Thought and Scholasticism. The Arguments for the Existence of God in Dutch Theology 1575–1650* (Leiden: Brill, 1982), p. 57. A different, less philosophically oriented reading of Ursinus is offered by J. P. Donnelly, 'Immortality and Method in Ursinus' Theological Ambiance', in D. Visser, ed., *Controversy and Conciliation. The Reformation and the Palatinate 1559–1583* (Allison Park: Pickwick, 1986), pp. 183–95. Donnelly suggests that in this respect Ursinus is closer to Vermigli than to (for example) Ursinus' successor in Heidelberg, Zanchius. See further J. P. Donnelly, *Calvinism and Scholasticism in Vermigli's Doctrine of Man and Grace* (Leiden: Brill, 1976).

matter with which theology deals: the 'positions' are 'methodically and briefly comprised' (*ordine et breviter comprehensas*). There is no hint here of the acute methodological self-awareness by which so much modern theology launches itself, no sense that problems of method have to reach a satisfactory conclusion before substantive discussion can proceed. 'Method' is mere technical organisation, and cannot of itself play anything other than an instrumental role in the presentation of the matter of the gospel. Third, therefore, where moderns might be facing anxieties about method, Ursinus is much more concerned for what might be called the right kind of vividness in theology: teaching must be undertaken in such a way that the substance of doctrine appears 'as it were painted before the eye'. *Rhetoric*, in other words, is what for Ursinus does the duty which in much mainstream modern theology is undertaken by *method*. And, fourth, this rhetoric is above all to be characterised by its stance beneath and its service of the scriptural texts. Theology is to have 'a kinde and manner of teaching and expression, as is both proper, plain, and agreeable with the style of the Prophets and Apostles'. That is, theological teaching, the discourse of Christian theological instruction, is to be judged appropriate when it allows the matter of theology – the prophetic and apostolic *sermo* – to stand before the hearer in its own inherent potency. Theology is to be proper (*propria*, that is, fitting to its object, not an attempt to manipulate that object or make it into something which it is not); it is to be clear or plain (*perspicua*, that is, it must allow the object of theology to appear and not obscure it with speculation or invention); and it is to be congruent with the traditions of prophetic and apostolic speech. In short: Christian theology is to manifest a modesty and transparency, a deferral to its object, which is the divine self-communication through Scripture.

It is for this reason that Ursinus goes on to describe a catechism as 'a summe of doctrine, delivered by the Prophets and Apostles, concerning faith and love in Christ. Or . . . a summe of doctrine of

Christianity, briefly, methodically, and plainly couched together'.[17] In practical terms, this means that doctrine serves Scripture, rather than the other way round. Scripture does not provide warrants for doctrinal proposals, simply because in Ursinus' model of theology, there is no such thing as a doctrinal proposal separate from exegesis. The nearest he comes to anything like a formal doctrinal statement is – as we shall see – in the idea of commonplaces. But there is little room in Ursinus' 'Oration' for dogmatics, and still less room for a conception of doctrine as an improvement upon Holy Scripture. There is simply the task of reading Holy Scripture, learning and teaching Scripture in such a way that godliness is promoted and the church more truthfully established as the kingdom of Jesus.

This can readily be seen by looking more closely at the way in which Ursinus conceives of the relation between doctrine and Scripture. Two things are especially worthy of note in this connection. First, theology is not invention but referral. '[I]t is not for us to invent opinions: but of necessity we must referre our selves, as it is, *Esay* 8.20, *to the Law and the Testimony*.'[18] The contrast is one between fabrication, producing ideas out of the mind's own inventiveness (*dogmata excogitare*) and 'referring ourselves' (*referre nos*) to Scripture, handing ourselves over to the given self-announcement of God. Theology is not a matter of starting *de novo*, but merely of tracing, heeding or indicating Scripture. Second, this makes explication necessary. To the outline of the scope of the scriptural gospel 'there must be added an exposition, which may be both a manifestation of the parts and method, and an interpretation of words and phrases'.[19] *Explicatio* (translated here as 'exposition') is a distinctly low-level enterprise, consisting in making plain (*monstratio*) the composition and structure of the biblical material, and in interpretation of its linguistic units. What for modern doctrinal theologians (even for some modern biblical scholars) would be preparatory work for the

---

[17] 'Oration', p. 4.   [18] Ibid.   [19] Ibid.

interpretative task is for Ursinus the culminating point of theological work.

Scripture and the theological school

Towards the end of the 'Oration', after a rather sharp attempt at refutation of the spiritualists' objections to the necessity of instruction in the church, Ursinus offers a portrait of the theological school. The presupposition of the whole account is the coinherence of *doctrina* and *pietas*. He writes thus: 'they that are brought up in the schools should be not only more learned, but also more godly. Which being so, let men acknowledge, that a school is a company according to God's ordinance, teaching and learning the doctrine necessary for mankind, concerning God and other good things; that the knowledge of God among men may not be extinguished, but the Church may be preserved, many may be made heirs of eternall life, discipline may be upheld, and men may have other honest benefits by the arts.'[20] The end of theology is practical knowledge of God, that is, knowledge which aims at the furtherance of the life of the Christian community, the salvation of humankind, and godly discipline. Theology is thus more a process of moral and spiritual training and an exercise in the promotion of common life than it is a scholarly discipline. 'Skills' are kept firmly tied to their end; in and of itself, the cultivation of learning is profitless because, unless directed to holiness, it is not only unattached but vicious. 'Therefore we swerve too far from our scope or marke, unlesse we be settled in this purpose, that we ought to be busily imployed in these Ant-hills and Bee-hives of Christ, not only to be more skilled in learning, but also more adorned with a good and holy conversation, that we may be more acceptable to God and men. And it is apparent in the Church, that all instruction, without the doctrine of godliness, is nothing else but an erring, and a withdrawing from God, from true good, true righteousness, true salvation. For

[20] Ibid., p. 11.

SCRIPTURE, THEOLOGY AND THE THEOLOGICAL SCHOOL

whatsoever we do not of faith, the holy spirit pronounceth as sinfull, vile, and condemned of God.'[21] And there are direct consequences here for the nature of the theological school, which is a common undertaking which orders its life in such a way as to stand beneath the divine imperative 'to search the Scriptures, to attend to reading, and rightly to divine the word of God'.[22] And 'because none can orderly and plainly distinguish, and lay open the speeches of the Prophets and Apostles, and the parts of Religion, without the instructions and exercises of the Schooles, who doth not see, with how neere a tye the study of godliness is knit unto the Schooles?'[23] In sum: 'That therefore which is the chiefe work amongst men, and cannot be performed of us without the help of the Schooles, we judge to be chief in the Schooles: namely, an understanding and interpretation of the Prophets and Apostles.'[24]

Loss of positivity and fragmentation of the curriculum

Why is it that the account of the nature of theology which surfaces in Ursinus does not generally commend itself to the theological guild in the institutions of higher learning? An adequate answer to that question would involve nothing less than a comprehensive history of modern understandings of the nature of theology and its institutional settings; but two lines of inquiry may be broached.

First, in formulating their self-understanding, the most intellectually and culturally prestigious theological institutions have generally followed the logic of the primacy of natural religion and universal reason, and as a consequence shifted from a positive to a critical understanding of the tasks of Christian theology. The removal from Christian theology of 'the scandal of positivity'[25] was a major factor

---

[21] Ibid., pp. 11f.   [22] Ibid., p. 12.   [23] Ibid.   [24] Ibid.

[25] The phrase is from G. Green, *Theology, Hermeneutics and Imagination. The Crisis of Interpretation at the End of Modernity* (Cambridge: Cambridge University Press, 2000), chapter 2; we may legitimately doubt if the antidote is the work of Hamann.

in the alienation of mainstream Christian theology from the peda-gogical vocation so finely set out by Ursinus, and (more seriously) from the scriptural *positum* which lay at the heart of his portrayal of the exercise of that vocation. In critical theology – the term is, of course, too undifferentiated, but it will serve as a marker – the peda-gogical or catechetical vocation is relegated to mere domestic status, for the task of critical theology is not instruction in the given truth of the church's confession of the gospel, but inquiry into the condi-tions of possibility of Scripture, church and gospel. Not only does this mean the estrangement of theology from the 'congregation' (for congregations are local confessional assemblies which cannot aspire to universal pertinence). It also means that what Ursinus saw as the chief theological task – the production of 'explications . . . agreeable to the speeches of the Prophets and Apostles' – no longer occupies centre stage. Descriptive exegesis can no longer support claims to truth, but must be grounded by critical theological inquiry.

In this connection, Hegel's remarks on the relation of theology to biblical exegesis in the *Lectures on the Philosophy of Religion* are ex-traordinarily instructive. Hegel clearly does not follow Kant in think-ing of the positivity of Scripture – and especially its Christological positivity – as merely a 'vivid mode of representing things',[26] an an-thropomorphic concession to our need for moral exemplars. Yet he shares Kant's reluctance to allow biblical exegesis to play any *fun-damental* role in presenting the truth of the Christian religion. His argument runs thus:

> Since the doctrines of the Christian religion are present in the Bible,
> they are thereby given in a positive fashion; and if they are subjectively
> appropriated, if spirit gives witness to them, this can happen in an
> entirely immediate fashion, with one's innermost being, one's spirit,
> one's thought, one's reason, being touched by them and assenting

[26] I. Kant, *Religion Within the Boundaries of Mere Reason*, in A.W. Wood and G. Di Giovanni, eds., *Religion and Rational Theology* (Cambridge: Cambridge University Press, 1996), p. 121.

to them. Thus the Bible is for Christians the basis, the fundamental basis, which has this effect on them, which strikes a chord within them, and gives firmness to their convictions.[27]

But, Hegel continues,

Human beings, because they are able to think, do not remain in the immediacy of assent and testimony, but also indulge in thoughts, in deliberation, in considerations concerning this immediate witness. These thoughts and considerations result in a developed religion; in its most highly developed form it is *theology* or scientific religion, whose content, as the witness of the spirit, is [also] known in scientific fashion.[28]

The contrasts there – between 'the immediacy of assent and testimony' and 'thoughts', and between 'immediate witness' and 'theology or scientific religion' – are indicative of the drifting apart of theology and exegesis (a severance which had already taken place, of course, in some measure at the hands of the divines of the post-Reformation period). Certainly there are pious folk, Hegel concedes, who 'hold exclusively to the Bible';[29] but '[t]heologians . . . they are not; such an attitude has nothing of a scientific, theological character'.[30] And so 'as soon as religion is no longer simply the reading and repetition of passages, as soon as what is called explanation or interpretation begins, as soon as the attempt is made by inference and exegesis to find out the *meaning* of the words in the Bible, then we embark upon the process of reasoning, reflection, thinking . . . As soon as these thoughts are no longer simply the words of the Bible, their content is given a form, more specifically, a logical form.'[31] If we probe Hegel a little more, we find that the distancing of theological thinking from exegesis is symptomatic of a further contrast

---

[27] G. W. F. Hegel, *Lectures on the Philosophy of Religion* (Berkeley: University of California Press, 1988), p. 399.
[28] Ibid., p. 400.   [29] Ibid.   [30] Ibid.   [31] Ibid.

between the merely external or customary and the internal or spiritual. Thinking is associated with the internal, and so ''[i]nsofar as theology is not a mere rehearsal of the Bible but goes beyond the words of the Bible and concerns itself with what kinds of feelings exist internally, it utilizes forms of thinking, it engages in thinking'.[32] Theology, therefore, if it is to be *thought*, must get beyond 'this contingent, arbitrary way of thinking', beyond 'the positive element'.[33] Christian doctrine is thus not – as in Ursinus – 'common places', an *index rerum* of Scripture, but the transformation of the *Vorstellungen* of positive Christianity into *Begriffe*: 'only its *form* is positive; its *content* is that of the spirit'.[34]

If Hegel is instructive, it is above all because he exemplifies how often modern accounts of the relation of theological reason to Holy Scripture are entangled in the dualism which, as we have seen, is so pervasive a feature of modern theological culture. The distancing of *Vorstellung* from *Begriff*, the relegation of texts to merely the matter of the life of unreflective piety, the identification of reason with that which is both most inward and most universal: all these features point to the way in which conceptions of theology have become dominated by an ideal of transcendental consciousness and reflectivity. When theology struggles to accommodate itself to that ideal, then guidance by texts and occupation of a place in the life of the communion of saints – that is, textual and social positivity – cannot be fundamentally determinative of the practices of theological reason.

A second line of reflection concerns the shift in the disciplinary arrangement of theology which further distances Ursinus' theological practice from our own conventions. The familiar modern pattern arranges theology by a four-fold division into biblical, historical, systematic-doctrinal and practical theology sub-disciplines.[35]

---

[32] Ibid., p. 401.   [33] Ibid., p. 402.   [34] Ibid.

[35] The history here is conveniently analysed in E. Farley, *Theologia. The Fragmentation and Unity of Theological Education* (Philadelphia: Fortress, 1983) and *The Fragility of Knowledge. Theological Education in the Church and the University* (Philadelphia: Fortress, 1988).

Ursinus himself mapped the theological task in a quite different way. There are, he says, 'three parts of the study of Divinity'. First, there is 'Catecheticall institution', defined as 'a summary and briefe explication of Christian doctrine'.[36] This is followed by 'an handling of Common places',[37] which is differentiated from 'institution' not in terms of its subject matter, but in terms of depth. The study of commonplaces covers the same ground as 'institution' and differs only in that it offers 'a larger explication of every point, and of hard questions together with their definitions, divisions, reasons, and arguments'.[38] Finally, there is 'the reading and diligent meditation of the Scripture, or holy Writ. And this is the highest degree of the study of Divinity, for which Catechisme and Common places are learned; to wit, that we may come furnished to the reading, understanding, and propounding of the holy Scripture.'[39] Three things might be noted about Ursinus' map. First, the distinctions he draws are not between different sub-disciplines but between different modes of engagement with the same unitary subject. Second, Holy Scripture is not simply one concern of theology, but that towards which all studies in divinity move. Third, the end of studies in divinity is clear: 'For Catechisme and Common places, as they are taken out of Scripture, and are directed by the Scripture as by their rule; so againe they conduct and lead us as it were by the hand into the Scripture.'[40]

One of the most important consequences of the replacement of this biblical and pastoral conception of theology by the four-fold pattern is the loss of the unity of theology as a coherent intellectual practice. The four-fold division can no longer provide the unity which a model such as that of Ursinus is given by its being centred on Scripture as the revelatory and pastoral heart of the entire theological enterprise. This is especially the case when the bonds between the practice of theology and the religious practices of the church are slackened. As this happens, each of the sub-disciplines

---

[36] 'Oration', p. 24.   [37] Ibid.   [38] Ibid.   [39] Ibid.   [40] Ibid.

tends to acquire its self-understanding, not from an overarching conception of the ends of theology as a particular instance of the ends of the church, but from cognate non-theological disciplines in the academy. Thus, for example, theological study of the Old Testament comes to enjoy a much closer relation to Near Eastern studies than it does to dogmatics. The effects of this are not difficult to discern: the difficulty of articulating a *theological* rationale for some parts of the theological curriculum; the professionalisation of the literatures and methods of inquiry of the sub-disciplines; above all, the danger of the fragmentation of theology into a collection of incoherent and pastorally marginal inquiries. And hence in terms of the place of Scripture in theology, the four-fold pattern therefore tends to make what on Ursinus' account is the centre of the entire operation – Holy Scripture as prophetic and apostolic testimony – into simply one of its constituent parts.

There is no inevitability about these inherited curricular arrangements and their rationale. They are not a fate; they are simply contingent dispositions of the matter whose momentum derives partly from their establishment in prestigious places of higher learning, partly from the cultural standing of the model of rational activity which undergirds them. Much is involved in resisting this momentum, however. Beyond the – scarcely imaginable – institutional and curricular change, two pieces of theoretical work are necessary. One is a genealogy of theological reason; the other is a dogmatic account of the office of theological reason in the church – an account, that is, which takes its bearings from the church's confession of the gospel. The genealogical work cannot be undertaken here;[41] but I may offer at least a thumbnail dogmatic sketch of the office of theology in order to round out this account of theology and Scripture.

---

[41] For the briefest of sketches, see my *Theological Theology* (Oxford: Clarendon Press, 1998).

Theology and Scripture

(1) Whatever its institutional location, Christian theology is properly an undertaking of the speaking and hearing church of Jesus Christ. It originates in the church's existence in the Word, and, like the church within which it undertakes its commission, it is governed and wholly referred to the Word or saving self-presence of God. In an important sense, theology is not an academic discipline generated by the pressure of the inquiring intellect; rather, it follows the same rule as all other thought, speech and action in the church, namely that it is brought about by the startling reality of the gospel of reconciliation. That gospel is not just the 'theme' or 'matter' of theology, as if the gospel were simply one more topic to which the inquiring human mind might choose to direct itself; rather, the gospel is that which brings theology into existence and holds it in being. As with the church, so with theology: its ontological ground, its *ratio essendi*, is the divine work of self-manifestation.

This means that Christian theology is, most generally described, an operation of reason in the economy of grace. The activity of theological reason is within the history of God's communicative and reconciling presence, reason, that is, enclosed by the realities of revelation and salvation. Theological reason comes to awareness of itself in so far as it is faced by the communicative self-presence of God; it is not in and of itself absolutely original or creative or free. Indeed, to claim that kind of originality, creativity or liberty for itself would be false to its calling and the office which it seeks to undertake.

Theological reason is not 'space-less', but located within the economy of grace, and therefore within the sphere of human fellowship in which the divine Word evokes the human act of faith – that is, within the sphere of the church: 'theological thinking and knowledge is possible only as *ecclesial thinking and knowledge*'.[42] Theology

---

[42] Bonhoeffer, *Act and Being. Transcendental Philosophy and Ontology in Systematic Theology* (Minneapolis: Fortress, 1996), p. 131.

is therefore an irreducibly positive science; it is reason directed to an *object* in a *place.* Yet great care has immediately to be exercised in making any such statement, for two reasons. First, the 'object' to which theological reason directs itself is subject, the free, personal, gratuitous presence of the holy God. And, second, the 'place' in which this object encounters us – that is, the church assembled by the Word and for the Word – is not simply a determinate cultural locale. The 'place' of the church is eschatological,[43] constituted by the terrifying aliveness of the risen one. Even in its reflective occupancy of that space, theological reason cannot proceed by any other way than that of being broken in its hearing of and reflection upon the divine Word. As Bonhoeffer puts it, 'Because theology turns revelation into something that exists, it may only be practised only where the living person of Christ is itself present and can destroy this existing thing or acknowledge it.'[44]

Theological reason, accordingly, is only properly responsible towards its origin when it is caught up by the Spirit's work of sanctification. Speaking can only proceed from hearing; and both hearing and speaking must be mortified by the Spirit if they are to be vivified and taken into the service of the gospel. If this is so, then what will characterise authentic theological reason will not be competence or invulnerability but rather 'holding fast in humility to the word that has been heard'.[45] Theological reason is not a mode of thinking in which we transcend and inspect from outside the struggle of faith to hear the Word; rather, theological reason participates in that struggle, sharing its temptations, subject to the same onslaught on wickedness as all other parts of human life, and subject also to the same promise of the Spirit's sanctification in the truth. Theological reason is reason put to death and made alive by the Spirit, reason transformed and renewed into attentiveness to, governance by and attestation of the divine Word.

[43] On this, see my essay 'Culture: The Shape of Theological Practice', *Stimulus* 6/4 (1998), pp. 2–9.
[44] Bonhoeffer, *Act and Being,* p. 131.   [45] Ibid.

(2) Because of all this, the exercise of theological reason, directed by the Word, is an *office* within the church. Kant was right to say that the 'biblical theologian' is a stranger to 'the free and open fields of private judgement', and is not contaminated by 'the ill-reputed spirit of freedom';[46] his mistake was to think that this means that the biblical theologian is thereby a stranger to reason. For Kant, 'reason' and 'office' are necessarily antithetical, because 'office' means submission to government and spells the end of freedom to evaluate. 'Reason is by nature free and admits of no command to hold something as true (no imperative "Believe!" but only a free *credo*).'[47] However, a Christian theological account of reason will want to disengage the exercise of reason from its associations with indeterminate liberty and the act of judgement. Such associations are deeply woven into the structure of the most commanding modern accounts of rational activity, including theological rationality. Yet for Christian theology they are unserviceable because they construe the world as the wrong kind of place and construe the life of reason in ways which are not fitting in the light of the gospel. The appeal of those conventions depends largely upon forceful moral commitment to a certain mode of critical inquiry. For Christian theology, however, if it is alert enough to give a Christian reading of its context and activities, those conventions lack the self-evident authority with which they are often credited. Realisation of this ought to give to Christian theology a measure of composure in undertaking its work in the absence of external justifications. Though Christian theology will certainly want to have its say in the conflict of the faculties, it will by no means feel itself compelled to wait for the resolution of that conflict before it can proceed. Rather than engaging in too much skirmishing about the nature of reason and its operations, an authentic Christian theology will simply go about its task with a measure of quiet determination, working under the tutelage and for the well-being of the

---

[46] I. Kant, *The Conflict of the Faculties*, in A.W. Wood and G. Di Giovanni, eds., *Religion and Rational Theology* (Cambridge: Cambridge University Press, 1996), p. 252.

[47] Ibid., p. 249.

spiritual community of which it is part and seeking thereby to fulfil its office.

In characterising more closely the 'official' character of theology, reference to the revelatory divine presence – that is, reference to the governance of the church by Word and Spirit – is all-important. Theological work is no less 'charismatic' or 'pneumatic' for being 'official'; 'office' is not simply the counterpart of regularity, stability and continuity. As an official activity, theology is appointed as one of the places in the life of the church where the church submits itself to judgement by the Word. Office does not reduce truth to routine; rather, it safeguards attention to prophecy:

> Theology is an act of repentant humility . . . This act exists in the fact that in theology the Church seeks again and again to examine itself critically as it asks itself what it means and implies to be a Church among men . . . The Church, too, lives under the judgement of God, as does the world. So, it cannot be otherwise but that the Church must critically examine itself, not according to its own wishes and standards but according to the standard which is identical with its basis of existence which is God's revelation, which, concretely, is the Holy Scriptures. It is this constant and ever-recurring necessity and demand for self-examination of the Church by the standard of the divine Word which is the peculiar function of theology in the Church.[48]

It is thus the office of theology in the church to serve the Word. Theology does not undertake the work of the Word itself; it is not competent to speak with authority the Word to which the church must submit, because theology is always and only the work of fragmentary and sinful reason. Theology, rather, *indicates* the presence and activity of the Word – that is, theology is awed testimony to the critical and consoling presence of God in the Spirit's power, set before the church in Holy Scripture. This indication is at the heart of

---

[48] K. Barth, 'Theology', in *God in Action* (Edinburgh: T. & T. Clark, 1936), pp. 44f.

the *critical* task of theology. Theology is critical, not because it follows the mandates of unformed and unrepentant reason, but because it is a place in the life of the church where the community is especially vigilant about its own capacity for idolatry. Theology is therefore a place where the crisis brought about by the activity of Word and Spirit is not *resolved* but rather especially *visible*. Yet even this work of indication is not a matter in which reason may operate as if it were simply extending itself into a sphere where it can legitimately claim a measure of expertise or resourcefulness. Like all speech in the church, theological speech only comes to have truthfulness, reliability and the capacity critically to illuminate in so far as it is made suitable – which means, in so far as it is sanctified to become a fitting 'custodian, catalogue and memorial of [the] Word'.[49]

This is why an account of theological reason will be Christianly deficient if it 'naturalises' reason's operations and declines to speak of reason as a sphere of God's activity. Theological reason is subject to the divine calling and the divine assistance. The notions of the calling of reason and of divine assistance of reason lift theology beyond either scepticism or retreat into apophasis. They secure for theology the basis on which it may proceed with a measure of – modest, self-distrustful yet real – confidence that rational thought and speech about God are possible because *made* possible by God. With this, as Ursinus puts it, 'we may despaire in nothing' in setting out to fulfil theology's office.[50]

Thus far, then, we have suggested that Christian theology takes its rise in the church's existence in the Word, and that theological reason is called and equipped to perform an office in the church. What more may be said of the specific content of that office? To what is theology called and for what undertaking is it equipped?

---

[49] D. Bonhoeffer, *Act and Being* (London: Collins, 1961), p. 145 (I follow the earlier translation here).
[50] Ursinus, 'Oration', p. 1.

(3) The office of theology is to assist in the edification of the church by guiding the church's reading of Holy Scripture. A number of consequences of this understanding of the theological task may be indicated.

First, the office of theology is in important respects a pastoral office, an exercise of pastoral responsibility in the communion of saints. It exercises this responsibility less directly than other offices in the church which are more specifically charged with the work of edification (that is, the ordered ministry of word and sacrament). And, like all office in the church, theology's pastoral activity is strictly subordinate to and dependent upon the divine work of edification, undertaken by the risen Christ who alone is 'the great shepherd of the sheep' (Heb. 13.20) and who alone equips the church 'with everything good' that it 'may do his will' (Heb. 13.21). Nevertheless, theology is a mode of the church's service of the gospel, and its end is the upbuilding of the Christian community. It is therefore more closely related to, for example, proclamation and catechesis than it is to history and philosophy. Whatever disciplinary and institutional shapes theological activity may assume must be subservient to the calling and end of theology, that is, to theology's establishment and authorisation by God for the upbuilding of the church, and to the location of theology in the community of the baptised.

Second, theology discharges its office by guiding the church's reading of Holy Scripture. Its guidance is modest. Theology does not direct the church's reading of Scripture in an imperious way, for then it would not only begin to play the part of an academic magisterium, but also arrogate to itself the work of the Holy Spirit. Nor does theology guide the church's reading of Holy Scripture by demanding that that reading conform to whatever criteria for the reading of texts are deemed normative in other reading communities – above all, the academic guild. Theology's guidance, in other words, is not offered from a position of relative distance from the church. Rather, theology guides the church by exemplifying submission to Holy Scripture as the *viva vox Dei*. It does not rule the church, or require the church to submit to its judgements; all that it offers is an exemplary instance of attentiveness to and deference before the gospel. Theology is therefore an exercise of the church's *hearing* of the gospel in Scripture, and only on that basis an exercise of teaching or guidance.

Third, accordingly, Holy Scripture is the centre of theology, not a subdivision within it, and all aspects of theological work are directed towards the reading of Holy Scripture, for – as Ursinus put it – 'the reading and diligent meditation of the Scriptures' is 'the highest degree of the study of Divinity'.[51] Reading Scripture is not only that from which theology proceeds, but also that to which theology is directed. Christian theology is the repetition in the movement of thought of attentive reading of Scripture.

This is particularly pertinent to the nature of dogmatic or systematic theology. The concepts and language of Christian dogmatics 'follow through' the act of reading Scripture; they are the transposition into reflective terms of what is learned from attentive reading. The aim of this transposition is not (as with Hegel) to effect a move from representation to concept, but simply to draw a map of the kinds of readings of the Bible which best promote the sovereignty of the gospel in the church. Theology is (to continue the cartographical metaphor) a projection which enables readers of Scripture to find their way around the biblical worlds. This is why (as Barth put it in his Anselm book) theological *intelligere* means nothing other than 'to read and ponder what has already been said';[52] that is, theology is 'no more than a deepened form of *legere*'.[53] To be sure, it is *deepened legere*: there is a proper level of theological reflectivity which is not to be collapsed into the more immediate activities of faith's apprehension of the *Credo*. But what is crucial here is that, as part of the understanding of faith, dogmatic theology is not superior to 'what has already been said'; nor is it about the business of inquiry into its possibility or necessity. Its task is more modest and restricted.

---

[51] 'Touching the Doctrine', in *The Summe of the Christian Religion*, p. 24.
[52] K. Barth, *Anselm: Fides Quaerens Intellectum* (London: SCM, 1960), p. 40.
[53] Ibid., p. 41.

'Dogmas', Hermann Diem suggested, 'arose in the process of ἀκοή.'[54] If that is so, then dogmatics has the function of enabling the church to be the *ecclesia audens*, assisting competent reading and reception of Scripture. As such, it is a summons to attentiveness, a reminder that, because the use of the Bible is always threatened by domestication, the church has always to *begin again* with Scripture. Theology is thus most properly an invitation to read and reread Scripture, to hear and be caught up by Scripture's challenge to a repentant, non-manipulative heeding of God's Word.

It is, therefore, of prime importance to avoid construing dogmatics as a set of improvements upon Scripture. The relative necessity of the theoretical language of dogmatics should not blind us to the fact that it is exposed to the 'heresy of paraphrase' – the assumption that theology, once formulated, effectively replaces the more rudimentary language forms of the Bible.[55] It is fatally easy to prefer the relatively clean lines of doctrine to the much less manageable, untheorised material of the Bible. But once we begin to do that, doctrine quickly becomes a way of easing ourselves of some permanently troubling tracts of Christian language: in effect, the rhetoric of dogma can serve to de-eschatologise the church's apprehension of the gospel. What is required in an account of dogma and its rhetoric is something much more light-weight, low-level and approximate, something therefore less likely to compete with or displace Scripture as the testimony to that around which Christian faith is organised. Thus modesty and transparency are the hallmarks of dogmatic rhetoric. In effect, this means that dogmatic theology operates best when it is a kind of gloss on Scripture – a discursive reiteration or indication of the truth of the Christian gospel as it is encountered in the Bible. Above all, what is required is an understanding of the

54 H. Diem, *Dogmatics* (Edinburgh: Oliver and Boyd, 1959), p. 301.
55 D. Tracy, *The Analogical Imagination* (London: SCM, 1981), p. 293, n. 57. See also G. Lindbeck's protest against 'translation theology' in 'Scripture, Consensus and Community', in R. J. Neuhaus, ed., *Biblical Interpretation in Crisis* (Grand Rapids: Eerdmans, 1989), pp. 87f.

nature of dogmatics which is self-effacing, in which its function is exhausted in the role it plays vis-à-vis Scripture. '[T]he Church's dogmatic activity, its attempts to structure its public and common language in such a way that the possibilities of judgement and renewal are not buried, must constantly be chastened by the awareness that it so acts in order to give place to the freedom of God – the freedom of God from the Church's sense of itself and its power, and thus the freedom of God to renew and absolve.'[56] If dogmatics has to do with 'giving place to the freedom of God', then its rhetoric must be modest enough to demonstrate and encourage attentiveness to Scripture.

Fourth, the rhetoric of theology is shaped by its end, namely the edification of the church through guidance in the reading of Scripture. The rhetoric of theology is the means whereby it positions itself in front of the listener or reader in such a way as to maximise its effect and thereby shape the reader in as deep and enduring a way as possible. 'Rhetoric' is used here in a very broad sense, referring not only to selection and use of language but also to the entire strategy of persuasion which a theologian adopts: genre, the use of authorities, conformity with or distance from shared assumptions and expectations, as well as modes of address. Because modern scholarly theology has adopted much of its self-understanding from the norms of cognate fields of inquiry (history, philosophy, social science) its rhetoric has often been assimilated to the standards of modern intellectual discourse. It has, accordingly, often been dominated by modes of discourse which appeal to the reader as one possessed of reason, reserved and unattached to any one particular version of reality, one for whom assent follows from sober weighing of evidence, cumulatively presented so as to appeal to the mind's judgement. Much theology in the classical mould was, by contrast, centrally (though not, of course, exclusively) concerned with the instruction, guidance and formation

---

[56] R. Williams, 'The Incarnation as the Basis of Dogma', in R. Morgan, ed., *The Religion of the Incarnation* (Bristol: Bristol Classical Press, 1989), p. 89.

of the disciples of Jesus Christ.[57] The effect of this on the rhetoric of theology is not simply to add pious flourishes to soften the severe lines of formal theological discussion. Still less is it a matter of abandoning theology to whatever practical issues happen to have found their way to the top of the church's agenda. It is rather a matter of recognition that, in following God's address of the church in Holy Scripture, theology cannot be anything other than a commendation of the gospel.

There are implications here for the genres of theological writing. A good deal of classical Christian theology was written as commentary, paraphrase or reflection upon major texts in the tradition – primarily biblical texts, but also by derivation credal or other writings of sufficient stature and durability to constitute permanently enriching statements of the gospel. Modern theology has largely lost touch with this genre.[58] The biblical commentary has by and large become the repository of linguistic, historical and literary comment; modern commentaries on credal texts are often little more than free reflection organised under the headings of the confession. One of the primary reasons for the decline of the genre of running paraphrase of or expansion upon classics (biblical or otherwise) is that the genre does not sit easily with the anti-statutory tendency of modernity which has deeply shaped scholarly rhetoric, and which makes these older genres scarcely recognisable as intellectual discourse. They are

---

[57] This has been called the 'salutarity' principle: theological doctrine is 'aretegenic' in that it has the pastoral task of seeking to cultivate virtue and thereby to edify. 'Christian doctrines function pastorally when a theologian unearths the divine pedagogy in order to engage the reader or listener in considering that life with the triune God facilitates dignity and excellence': E. Charry, *By the Renewing of Your Minds. The Pastoral Function of Christian Doctrine* (Oxford: Oxford University Press, 1997), p. 18; see further S. Jones, *Calvin and the Rhetoric of Piety* (Louisville: Westminster John Knox Press, 1995) and W. Placher, *The Domestication of Transcendence* (Louisville: Westminster John Knox Press, 1996), pp. 52–68.

[58] On the significance of commentary, see P. Griffiths, *Religious Reading. The Place of Reading in the Practice of Religion*, (Oxford: Oxford University Press, 1999) pp. 77–97, and especially J. B. Henderson, *Scripture, Canon, and Commentary. A Comparison of Confucian and Western Exegesis* (Princeton: Princeton University Press, 1991).

deliberately unoriginal; they take us immediately *in medias res* and do not feel excessively anxious to start *de novo*; they do not accept that 'recital' and 'creativity' are necessarily antithetical.[59] They demonstrate rather little interest in giving an account of the historical genesis of that upon which they comment. Their relationship to the language of the Bible and its derivative dialects is prior to their relation to the language of high culture or philosophy. And they are unsystematic, in that they eschew reorganising their material, preferring to let its own logic stand without submitting it to pressure to conform to external schemes. Above all, they are transparent to Holy Scripture, whose potency as prophetic and apostolic discourse they seek simply to indicate. Calvin says this in his address to the reader which prefaces his commentary on the psalter:

> I have not only preserved throughout a plain and simple manner of teaching, but that all ostentation might be the further removed, I have for the most part abstained from refutations which presented a more free scope for plausible display. Nor have I ever touched upon opposite opinions save when there was danger lest by keeping silence I might leave my readers doubtful and in the briars. Nor does it escape me how much sweeter it is to supply materials for ambitious display, by bringing together a mass of things of every sort. But nothing was of more importance with me than to consult for the edifying of the church.[60]

There are few more compact statements of the office of theology in the church of the Word.

The preceding sketch of the nature of theology and of the theological school and their relation to Holy Scripture is frankly utopian, and may therefore be thought to be irresponsible. But utopias may not always be fantasy; they may be an attempt to reach towards the

---

[59] See here the comments on the florilegium in J. Pelikan, *The Vindication of Tradition* (New Haven: Yale University Press, 1984), pp. 74f.

[60] J. Calvin, 'John Calvin to the Godly Reader Sends Greeting', in *A Commentary on the Psalms*, vol. 1 (London: Clarke, 1965), pp. 23f.

eschatological, and to conceive of the forms which might be taken by convertedness. A utopian account of theological reason is a bid to register two things: that only through its devastation can reason be renewed, and that the end of reason's devastation is nothing less than its renewal. Taking that devastation and renewal seriously will almost inevitably mean that theology will find itself moving to the edge of the modern university. In contexts committed to the sufficiency of natural reason (or at least to the unavailability of anything other than natural reason), theology will have something of the scandalous about it. Ultimately, what is scandalous about Christian theology is that it is a work of reason which can only fulfil its office if it bears the marks of God's destruction of the wisdom of the wise and the cleverness of the clever. *If* it bears those marks . . . for there is no assurance that theology will bear them. One of the perennial temptations of the theologian is to distance theological reason from the absolute breach between divine and human wisdom, to set theological reason under a sign other than baptism. To resist this, to live out theological existence under the sign of baptism, requires that in all the activities of theological reason there be traced a two-fold work of God: judgement and the giving of life. Judgement is the work of making foolish the world's wisdom; the gift of life includes the fact that Jesus Christ is truly the wisdom by which theological reason is sustained.

Baptism is the origin and permanent condition of theological reason. Existing under this sign, theology inevitably encounters some distress in the modern research university. But the distress does not necessarily bespeak the need for theology's withdrawal from public institutions. If theology needs to be healthily critical of the presumption that such institutions of higher learning are the only fitting locations for responsible intellectual activity, it should be no less sceptical of the presumption that the sanctification of theology will necessarily be secured by its separation from such contexts. Questions about the settings of the life of theological reason – like questions about its methods – are prudential decisions which must be governed both by judgements about particular circumstances and by clear discernment of the ends of theological reason, ends which are determined not simply from wider cultural conventions but from the economy of God.

What is clear is that the kind of theology whose defining activity is exegetical reason needs to be ready to take its share of the embarrassment and censure which accompany its exile. Survival under the afflictions of exile involves many practices, of which two are primary. One is fellowship under the Word – that is, common life led by delight in the common reality of the communicative presence of God. Reason requires *koinonia*.[61] The second is that fundamental act by which the common life of reason appeals for its cleansing, protection and truthfulness, namely prayer: 'May the Lord grant that we may study the heavenly mysteries of his wisdom, making true progress in religion to his glory and our upbuilding' (Calvin).

[61] On the interdependence of rational activity and social relations, see A. MacIntyre, *Dependent Rational Animals. Why Human Beings Need the Virtues* (London: Duckworth, 1999).

In Place of a Conclusion

'Therefore, brethren, may this be the result of my admonition, that you understand that in raising your hearts to the Scriptures (when the gospel was sounding forth, "In the beginning was the Word, and the Word was with God, and the Word was God", and the rest that was read), you were lifting your eyes to the mountains, for unless the mountains said these things, you would not find out how to think of them at all. Therefore from the mountains came your help, that you even heard of these things; but you cannot yet understand what you have heard. Call for help from the Lord, who made heaven and earth; for the mountains were enabled only so to speak as not of themselves to illuminate, because they themselves are also illuminated by hearing. Thence John, who said these things, received them – he who lay on the Lord's breast, and from the Lord's breast drank in what he might give us to drink. But he gave us words to drink. Thou oughtest then to receive understanding from the source from which he drank who gave thee to drink; so that thou mayest lift up thine eyes to the mountains from whence shall come thine aid, so that from thence thou mayest receive, as it were, the cup, that is, the word, given thee to drink; and yet, since thy help is from the Lord, who made heaven and earth, thou mayest fill thy breast from the source from which he filled his; whence thou saidst, "My help is from the Lord, who made heaven and earth": let him, then, fill who can. Brethren, this is what I have said: Let each one lift up his heart in the manner that seems fitting, and receive what is spoken. But perhaps you will say that I am more present to you than God. Far be such a thought from you! He is much more present to you; for I appear to your eyes, he presides over your consciences. Give me then your ears, give him your hearts, that you may fill both. Behold, your eyes, and those your bodily senses, you lift up to us; and yet not to us, for we are not of those mountains, but to the gospel itself, to the evangelist himself: your hearts, however, to the Lord to be filled. Moreover, let each one so lift up as to see what he lifts up, and whither. What do I mean by saying, "what he lifts up, and whither?" Let him see to it what sort of a heart he lifts up, because it is to the Lord he lifts it up, lest, encumbered by a load of fleshly pleasure, it fall ere ever it is raised. But does each one see that he bears a burden of flesh? Let him strive by continence to purify that which he may lift up to God. For "Blessed are the pure in heart, because they shall see God.""[1]

---

[1] Augustine, *Homilies on the Gospel of John* i.vii.

Bibliography

Abraham, W. J. *Canon and Criterion in Christian Theology. From the Fathers to Feminism* (Oxford: Clarendon Press, 1998)

   The Divine Inspiration of Holy Scripture (Oxford: Oxford University Press, 1981)

Appel, N. *Kanon und Kirche* (Paderborn: Bonifacius, 1964)

Barr, J. *Holy Scripture. Canon, Authority, Criticism* (Oxford: Clarendon Press, 1983), pp. 105–26

Barth, K. *Church Dogmatics* I/2 (Edinburgh: T. & T. Clark, 1956)

   'Revelation', in *God in Action* (Edinburgh: T. & T. Clark, 1936), pp. 3–19

Bavinck, H. *Our Reasonable Faith* (Grand Rapids: Eerdmans, 1956)

Bayer, O. *Gott als Autor* (Tübingen: Mohr, 1999)

Berkouwer, G. C. *Holy Scripture* (Grand Rapids: Eerdmans, 1975)

Bonhoeffer, D. 'Vergegenwärtigung neutestamentlicher Texte', in *Gesammelte Schriften*, vol. III (Munich: Kaiser, 1966), pp. 303–24

Braaten, C. and Jenson, R., eds., *Reclaiming the Bible for the Church* (Grand Rapids: Eerdmans, 1995)

Cantwell Smith, W. *What is Scripture? A Comparative Approach* (London: SCM, 1993)

Dalferth, I. U. 'Die Mitte ist außen. Anmerkungen zum Wirklichkeitsbezug evangelischer Schriftauslegung', in C. Landmesser et al., eds., *Jesus Christus als die Mitte der Schrift. Studien zur Hermeneutik des Evangeliums* (Berlin: de Gruyter, 1997), pp. 173–98

   'Von der Vieldeutigkeit der Schrift und der Eindeutigkeit des Wortes Gottes', in R. Ziegert, ed., *Die Zukunft des Schriftprinzips* (Stuttgart: Deutsche Bibelgesellschaft, 1994), pp. 155–73

Dehn, G. *Man and Revelation* (London: Hodder and Stoughton, 1936)

Ebeling, G. 'The Significance of the Critical Historical Method for Church and Theology', in *Word and Faith* (London; SCM, 1963), pp. 17–61

Fackre, G. *The Doctrine of Revelation. A Narrative Interpretation* (Edinburgh: Edinburgh University Press, 1997)

Farley, E. *Ecclesial Reflection. An Anatomy of Theological Method* (Philadelphia: Fortress Press, 1982)

Fowl, S. *Engaging Scripture* (Oxford: Blackwell, 1998)

Fowl, S., ed., *The Theological Interpretation of Scripture* (Oxford: Blackwell, 1997)

Fowl, S. and Jones, G. *Reading in Communion* (Grand Rapids: Eerdmans, 1991)

Grafton, A. *Defenders of the Text. The Traditions of Scholarship in an Age of Science, 1450–1800* (Cambridge, Mass.: Harvard University Press, 1991)

Green, G. *Imagining God. Theology and the Religious Imagination* (San Francisco: Harper and Row, 1989)

    Theology, Hermeneutics and Imagination. The Crisis of Interpretation at the End of Modernity (Cambridge: Cambridge University Press)

Griffiths, P. *Religious Reading. The Place of Reading in the Practice of Religion* (Oxford: Oxford University Press, 1999)

Gunton, C. *A Brief Theology of Revelation* (Edinburgh: T. & T. Clark, 1995)

Healy, N. 'Hermeneutics and the Apostolic Form of the Church: David Demson's Question', *Toronto Journal of Theology* 17 (2001), pp. 17–32

Henderson, J. B. *Scripture, Canon and Commentary. A Comparison of Confucian and Western Exegesis* (Princeton: Princeton University Press, 1991)

Heppe, H. *Reformed Dogmatics* (London: George Allen and Unwin, 1950)

Herms, E. 'Was haben wir an der Bibel? Versuch einer Theologie des christlichen Kanons', *Jahrbuch für biblische Theologie* 12 (1998), pp. 99–152

Horton, M. S. *Covenant and Eschatology. The Divine Drama* (Louisville: WJKP, 2002)

Huizing, K. *Homo legens. Vom Ursprung der Theologie im Lesen* (Berlin: de Gruyter, 1996)

Jasper, D. *Readings in the Canon of Scripture* (Basingstoke: Macmillan, 1995)

Jeanrond, W. *Text and Interpretation as Categories of Theological Thinking* (Dublin: Gill and Macmillan, 1988)

Theological Hermeneutics. Development and Significance (London: SCM, 1988)

Jeffrey, D. Lyle *People of the Book. Christian Identity and Literary Culture* (Grand Rapids: Eerdmans, 1996)

Jenson, R. *Systematic Theology*, vol. 1 (Oxford: Oxford University Press, 1997)

Kelsey, D. 'The Bible and Christian Theology', *Journal of the American Academy of Religion* 48 (1980), pp. 385–402

The Uses of Scripture in Recent Theology (London: SCM, 1975)

Khoury, A. T. and Muth, L., eds., *Glauben durch Lesen? Für eine christliche Lesekultur* (Freiburg: Herder, 1990)

Kort, W. *'Take, Read'. Scripture, Textuality, and Cultural Practice* (University Park: Pennsylvania State University Press, 1996)

Körtner, U. H. J. *Der inspirierter Leser. Zentrale Aspekte biblischer Hermeneutik* (Göttingen: Vandenhoeck und Ruprecht, 1994)

Law, D. *Inspiration* (London: Continuum, 2001)

Levering, M., ed., *Rethinking Scripture* (Albany: SUNY Press, 1989)

Lindbeck, G. 'Barth and Textuality', *Theology Today* 46 (1986), pp. 361–76

'The Church's Mission to a Postmodern Culture', in F. Burnham, ed., *Postmodern Theology. Christian Faith in a Pluralist World* (San Francisco: Harper, 1988), pp. 37–55

The Nature of Doctrine (London: SPCK, 1984)

'Scripture, Consensus, and Community', in R. J. Neuhaus, ed., *Biblical Interpretation in Crisis* (Grand Rapids: Eerdmans, 1989), pp. 74–101

Lundin, R., ed., *Disciplining Hermeneutics* (Grand Rapids: Eerdmans, 1997)

Moberly, R. W. L. *The Bible, Theology and Faith* (Cambridge: Cambridge University Press, 2000)

Morgan, R. with Barton, J. *Biblical Interpretation* (Oxford: Oxford University Press, 1988)

Muller, R. A. *Post-Reformation Reformed Dogmatics 2: Holy Scripture* (Grand Rapids: Baker, 1992)

Pannenberg, W. *Systematic Theology*, vol. 1 (Edinburgh: T. & T. Clark, 1991)

Preus, J. Samuel *Spinoza and the Irrelevance of Biblical Authority* (Cambridge: Cambridge University Press, 2001)

Preus, R. *The Inspiration of Scripture. A Study of the Theology of the Seventeenth Century Lutheran Dogmaticians* (Edinburgh: Oliver and Boyd, 1957)

Reventlow, H. G. *The Authority of the Bible and the Rise of the Modern World* (London: SCM, 1980)

Rowland, C. 'Christology, Controversy and Apocalypse: New Testament Exegesis in the Light of the Work of William Blake', in D. G. Horrell and C. M. Tuckett, eds., *Christology, Controversy and Community* (Leiden: Brill, 2000), pp. 355–78

Schlink, E. *Ökumenische Dogmatik. Grundzüge* (Göttingen: Vandenhoeck und Ruprecht, 1983)

Schneiders, S. *The Revelatory Text. Interpreting the New Testament as Sacred Scripture* (San Francisco: Harper and Row, 1991)

Senarclens, J. de *Heirs of the Reformation* (London: SCM, 1963)

G. Siegwalt, 'Le canon biblique et la révélation', in *Le christianisme, est-t-il une religion du livre?* (Strasbourg: Faculté de théologie protestante, 1984), pp. 39–56

Smith, J. K. A. *The Fall of Interpretation. Philosophical Foundations for a Creational Hermeneutic* (Downers Grove: InterVarsity Press, 2000)

Spykman, G. *Reformational Theology. A New Paradigm for Doing Dogmatics* (Grand Rapids: Eerdmans, 1992)

Thiemann, R. *Revelation and Theology. The Gospel as Narrated Promise* (Notre Dame: Notre Dame University Press, 1985)

Torrance, T. F. 'The Deposit of Faith', *Scottish Journal of Theology* 36 (1983), pp. 1–28.

   Divine Meaning (Edinburgh: T. & T. Clark, 1995)

   The Hermeneutics of John Calvin (Edinburgh: Scottish Academic Press, 1988)

Vanhoozer, K. *First Theology. God, Scripture and Hermeneutics* (Leicester: Apollos, 2002)

   Is There a Meaning in This Text? (Grand Rapids: Zondervan, 1998)

Wagner, F. 'Auch der Teufel zitiert die Bibel. Das Christentum zwischen Autoritätsanspruch und Krise des Schriftprinzips', in R. Ziegert, ed., *Die Zukunft des Schriftprinzips* (Stuttgart: Deutsche Bibelgesellschaft, 1994), pp. 236–58

Ward, T. *Word and Supplement. Speech Acts, Biblical Texts, and the Sufficiency of Scripture* (Oxford: Oxford University Press, 2002)

Watson, F. *Text, Church and World* (Edinburgh: T. & T. Clark, 1994)

Weber, O. *Foundations of Dogmatics*, vol. 1 (Grand Rapids: Eerdmans, 1981)

Welker, M. 'Sozio-metaphysische Theologie und Biblische Theologie. Zu Eilert Herms: "Was haben wir an der Bibel?"', *Jahrbuch für biblische Theologie* 13 (1999), pp. 309–22

Wenz, A. *Das Wort Gottes – Gericht und Rettung. Untersuchungen zur Autorität der Heiligen Schrift in Bekenntnis und Lehre der Kirche* (Göttingen: Vandenhoeck und Ruprecht, 1996)

Williams, R. 'The Discipline of Scripture', in *On Christian Theology* (Oxford: Blackwell, 2000), pp. 44–59

Wolterstorff, N. *Divine Discourse* (Cambridge: Cambridge University Press, 1995)

Wood, C. *The Formation of Christian Understanding* (Philadelphia: Westminster, 1981)

Index

accommodation 22, 26
adoptionism 24
apostolicity 50–1, 64
Augustine 61, 91–2, 94
authority 52–7

Barr, J. 103–4
Barth, K. 15, 16, 23, 80, 82–3, 85, 129
Bavinck, H. 25, 100
Berkouwer, G. C. 25, 58–60
Bethge, E. 82
Bonhoeffer, D. 69, 78–85, 105, 124
Bultmann, R. 80, 104

Calov, A. 69, 70
Calvin, J. 32, 44–5, 56, 60–2, 69, 74–8, 90,
    113, 133, 135
canon, canonisation 30, 58–67
    as confession, 62–3
    as submission, 63–4
    as retrospection, 64
    as obligation, 64–5
catechesis 108–9, 112–16, 121, 122
church 7–8, 32, 42–67, 71, 123–4,
    126–9
Congar, Y. 51

Dalferth, I. U. 7–8
Dehn, G. 2–3
deism 36
Derrida, J. 100
Descartes, R. 73

dictation 39
Diem, H. 130
doctrine 68, 109
dogmatics 129–31
Dooyeweerd, H. 100
dualism 10, 19–22, 26–8, 35

Ebeling, G. 104
election 27
epistemology 12–13, 17, 32, 33
exegesis 3, 119–20

faith 32, 44–5, 50, 66
fellowship 15–16, 70–1
Folkert, K. 65

gospel 123
grace 71
Grant, G. 104
Green, G. 96–9

Hegel, G. W. F. 118–20, 129
Heppe, H. 31
Heidelberg Catechism 107
hermeneutics 99–100
holiness 27
Holy Spirit 17, 21, 24, 26–31, 33, 35–40,
    44–5, 48, 52, 55, 56, 60, 62, 71, 82,
    87–95, 101, 108, 111, 124, 126–7
Horton, M. 39
Huizing, K. 100–1
hypostatic union 22–3, 26

imagination 96–7
incarnation 23
inspiration 8–10, 20, 26, 30–9, 41, 55
interpretation 30, 86, 97–9, 106

Jeanrond, W. 29, 95–6
Jenson, R. 63
Jesus Christ 11–17, 21, 38, 44, 48, 50, 58–60, 66, 81–2, 88, 89, 91–2, 101, 108–9, 124, 128

Kant, I. 54, 56, 104, 111, 118, 125
Kierkegaard, S. 90
Kort, W. 75
Kuyper, A. 100

Law, D. 34–5, 100
Lindbeck, G. 48–50
Luther, M. 104

Macquarrie, J. 34–5
Marsh, C. 80
Martensen, H. 33, 35
means of grace 24, 26
mediation 10, 25, 59
Melanchthon, P. 107, 113
mortification 88–90

Niebuhr, H. R. 57
nominalism 19, 54

perspicuity 81, 91–101, 106
Preus, R. 39
providence 10

reading, reader 68, 109, 128–9
reason 108, 123, 127, 134–5
reconciliation 16, 87–8, 108
revelation 9, 11–17, 31–3, 40, 57, 91
rhetoric of theology 131–3

sacrament 9
sanctification 8–10, 17–30, 41, 124
Schleiermacher, F. D. E. 60
Schopenhauer, A. 69, 72–3
servant-form of Scripture 25–8
Siegwalt, G. 15
sin 87–8
Smith, J. K. A. 99–100
Smith, W. C. 6–8
soteriology 9, 17, 35, 40, 52
Spinoza, B. 19
Spykman, G. 22

testimony 23–6
theology, theological school 116–22
theology and Scripture 123–35
tradition 51–2
Trinity 6, 8–9, 12–14, 17–18, 21, 43, 44, 50, 70

Ursinus, Z. 107–18, 120–1, 127, 129

Vatican II 93
vivification 88–91

Westcott, B. F. 30
Word of God 14, 35, 44–7, 50–2, 57, 66, 86–7, 92–3, 123, 124, 126–7

Zwingli, U. 101–4